Corvettes

The Cars that Created the Legend

Corvettes

The Cars that Created the Legend

Written and Photographed by
Dennis Adler

KRAUSE PUBLICATIONS

Published by

 **krause
publications**

700 East State Street
Iola, Wisconsin 54990-0001

Please call or write for our free catalog of publications. Our toll-free number to place an order or to obtain a free catalog is (800) 258-0929. Please use our regular business telephone (715) 445-2214 for editorial comment and further information.

Library of Congress Catalog Number: 95-77322
ISBN: 0-87341-367-9
Printed in the United States of America

To Jeanne

'Twas a Corvette first caught my eye,
But the driver who stole my heart.

Contents

About the Author

Recognized as one of the leading automotive photographers and writers in the country, Dennis Adler's work has appeared in publications ranging from *Motor Trend*, *Road & Track* and *AutoWeek*, to *European Car*, the *Robb Report*, *Car Collector & Car Classics*, *Automobile Quarterly*, *Popular Mechanics*, *Super Chevy*, *Popular Hot Rodding*, *Forbes*, and the *DuPont Registry*.

A native Californian now living in the central Pennsylvania countryside, he has served on the editorial staffs of more than a dozen national magazines during his 20 year career, including 18 years as a contributing editor to *Car Collector & Car Classics*.

His photographs have graced hundreds of magazine covers, are framed on the walls of corporate offices, and during the late eighties, he did much of the new product photography for the Chevrolet Motor Car Division of General Motors, including the famous Corvette "ZR-1 Seascape" photo used by Chevrolet in 1989.

Mr. Adler is presently East Coast Editor of *European Car*, Senior Editor of *Car Collector & Car Classics*, Contributing Editor/Autos and Automotive Historian for the *Robb Report*, and for more than a decade, Contributing Editor to *The Star*—the official publication of the Mercedes-Benz Club of America. A leading authority on the marque, he has written more than 100 articles on Mercedes-Benz models and two books on the subject, *Mercedes-Benz 300SL*, published in 1994, and his latest, *Mercedes-Benz: 110 Years of Excellence*, celebrating the marque's 110th anniversary. He is currently at work on *Cars of the Fifties—A Nostalgic Look at America's Big Steel Era*.

Acknowledgments

I don't believe that anyone really writes a Corvette book. At best we repeat the history that has become subject to some well meant exaggerations; great topics inspire us to commit such transgressions. No one can write a book on the subject without following in the footsteps of so many who have trod this path before. One could not capably write even a pictorial history such as this without referring to Karl Ludvigsen's *Corvette—America's Star-Spangled Sports Car,* or Richard Langworth's superb reference work, *The Complete Book of Corvette. The Genuine Corvette Black Book* by Michael Antonick is another invaluable reference for cross-checking historical data. Moreover, the men of Corvette (and my conversations with them over the years), most notably Zora Arkus-Duntov, Dave McLellan and Jim Perkins—who by all account is the most enthusiastic leader Chevrolet has had since the days of Ed Cole—have played a significant role in the making of this book. Zora once told me, while posing with the Corvette Grand Sport prototype, that the cars have been most of his life. In some small way, he has been a part of most of ours through the Corvette.

I would be greatly remiss to overlook years of friendship with Chip Miller, perhaps the most avid Corvette enthusiast in America, who has been a continual source of ideas, contacts, and cars throughout the past year spent producing this book. And I would be remiss if I did not thank all of the owners who contributed their time by making their cars available to me. It would take pages to name them all, but I hope that when they see the final result of long photo sessions, late night phone calls, and weekends spent away from home, each will find in the photographs of their cars a satisfaction we all share in perpetuating the Corvette's role in American automotive history. To one and all my heartfelt thanks and appreciation.

My own personal interest in Corvettes, like so many of my friends, dates back to the 1960s. The Corvette was one of those cars that left a lasting impression from the very beginning. It was probably *Route 66* that first made me think of owning a Corvette and touring free-spirited across the country like Martin Milner and George Maharis, aka Tod Stiles and Buzz Murdock—but then again I was only 13 and totally oblivious to the impracticality of such a life, however romantic it may have seemed in 1961.

It would take 25 years before a new Corvette found its way into my garage. Of course, along the way I had the opportunity to test drive and write about more than two decade's worth of new and old models alike.

Of all the Corvettes I have ever had the pleasure of driving, the most memorable is the ZR-1. In 1989, when I was photographing prototype models for Chevrolet, I was handed the keys to one of the first pre-production models, then still known internally as the LT-5, a car which surprised me as much with its unparalleled performance as its subtle but effective distinction from other Corvettes. It was and still remains my favorite contemporary model, second only in favor to the 1962 Corvette. The last time I drove a Corvette ZR-1, I was dancing it through rain at Watkins Glen trying to follow Rusty Wallace's line, no mean feat, since he had pointed out during an earlier session around the track that, "this is where I lost it last week. . ." The last turn before the front straight turned out to be where I lost it, as well.

Being a test driver has its perks. You get to go around the world at someone else's expense, stay in the finest hotels, eat the best regional foods, and drive the most expensive automobiles put on this planet. And best of all, someone is paying you to do it! These, however, are not the thoughts going through your mind when the view through the windshield changes from wet pavement to wet grass, and then to wet corrugated steel, tire stacks, and hay bales.

I had made a mental error at the apex of the turn and sent the ZR-1 spinning through the water like one of those cars you see in a slow motion commercial. Only I wasn't controlling the graceful spin, I was just along for the ride. When everything came to a stop, the ZR-1 was barely scathed, and after a quick walk around the car, it was evident that the greatest damage had been done to my self esteem. You see, I was driving the *camera car* and every excruciating second of my run was on videotape!

Corvettes have played a part in my life during good times and bad, as they have in the lives of so many others. There is a camaraderie among owners that transcends age, income, and education; in fact, there are very few cars in the world that can bring people together with such otherwise diverse interests as the Corvette. It has become an American institution in which everyone involved can take pride, from the Chevrolet engineering staff right down to the guys who wash the cars off every morning at your local Chevy dealer. They are all part of the Corvette family—something uniquely American.

—Dennis Adler

Foreword

The Corvette's Role in American Automotive History

Chip Miller

Back in the early sixties, I started dreaming about cars that would some day be collectible—cars that I would have to own. Most of the time, I dreamed with my eyes open. In truth, I was possessed by my dream.

Think back, if you can, thirty years ago. Collector cars at the time fell into two categories; they were either early 1900s antiques like the Ford Model T or thirties era classics like the Duesenberg and Packard. Fifties and sixties cars were considered "drivers," not collector cars. In my mind, however, they were much more.

I first noticed the Corvette in a 1956 issue of *Sports Illustrated*. There, opposite some long forgotten article was a full-page ad showing what I still believe to be one of the best looking cars ever designed.

From that 1956 model, through the introduction of quad head-lights, freshened styling in '61, and the first 327 small block in '62, I loved Corvettes more than any other car. When Chevrolet came out with the Sting Ray Coupe in 1963, I fell in love all over again. About the time the big block was introduced in mid-1965, my dreams of Corvette ownership started. Sure, I sometimes strayed—thoughts of Cobras, 300SLs, Porsches, and Ferraris, cars that have also become collectible, but the Corvette reigned in my mind.

Why? It was everything! Design, power, American, Fiberglas, American—okay, two votes for its ancestry, because Corvettes were show-ing the world what an American automaker could do with a European concept. The Corvette had become the only American sports car by the late fifties. Ford had abandoned the Thunderbird two-seater in 1958.

In the America of my youth, Chevrolet was number one in sales by a great margin. Every town had a Chevrolet dealership and most had a Corvette on the showroom floor. The ultimate display of "cool" in the early sixties was being seen in a 'Vette.

When you talk about Corvette history, you're also talking about great strides in American automotive performance and technology. If it was new, Chevrolet introduced it on the Corvette. The '57 model year is a typical example: 4-speed transmission, positraction rear, heavy duty racing suspension, fuel injection, and a 283 cid V8 developing 283 horsepower. Before the Corvette, one horsepower per cubic inch had been unheard of in an American car.

The late fifties and early sixties were distinguished by improvements in design and heavy duty racing options like metallic brakes, off-road exhaust, heavy duty steering and a 24 gallon fuel tank. The mid-sixties saw the introduction of big blocks, disc brakes, and Corvette racing. Under the guidance of Zora Arkus-Duntov, Chevrolet bared its teeth, and when a "factory" high performance part was needed, Mr. Duntov created it! Chevy's efforts started at Daytona Beach in 1956 and Corvettes dominated their classes in Sports Car Club of America (SCCA) racing throughout the fifties and early sixties.

In 1956 Dr. Dick Thompson won the Class C Production racing title. In 1957 Dr. Thompson (co-driving with Gaston Audrey) won the 12-hour at Sebring on his way to the Class B Production racing title. J. E. Rose secured the B Sports national title. In 1958 and 1959 Jim Jeffords took the points championship in Class B Production. Bob Johnson took the same title in 1960 with Dick Thompson winning it in 1961. In 1962 it was Don Yenko taking the B Production crown while Thompson took the A Production points championship.

By 1962 cubic inch displacement had been increased to 327 and an independent rear suspension was introduced the following year. To go racing, all one had to check off on the order blank was the RPO Z06 option. Unfortunately for the Corvettes, a man by the name of Carroll Shelby also had Duntov's vision of dominating the race tracks of the world. Shelby's Cobra was much lighter and more nimble. Duntov set his sights higher and bested Shelby's Fords with the Corvette Grand Sport. If Chevrolet hadn't pulled the plug on the Grand Sport project (only five were built) the outcome might have been different. History shows Cobras broke Corvettes' great string of SCCA championships in 1963 and continued to dominate for some years after, but for one brief season, Duntov's Grand Sports and the Mecom racing team took all the venom out of the Cobra.

The L-88 came along from 1967 to 1969 and helped the Corvette achieve a goodly number of wins; however, it wasn't until the mid-eighties that Corvettes would totally dominate SCCA racing. So much so, SCCA told Corvettes to go play in their own sandbox—and the Corvette Challenge was created! This series was good for the racers—many of whom went on to dominate in the Trans Am and Indy Car ranks. It was also good for Chevrolet—they used the series for publicity and as a test-bed to improve the Corvette.

Racing has played an important role in the Corvette's history but the ultimate visibility of the car has always been on the roads of America. Corvettes capture the most attention on the asphalt with the tires and wheels turning high rpms. They have always been a thing of beauty, whether they were one day young or 40 years old!

The impact of this car on the collector hobby is a success story in itself. Most of the earlier cars have since been retired from street use. Some are on blocks awaiting restoration, some have survived the years without need of restoration, and many have been rebuilt to like-new perfection.

To me, and so many others, Corvette ownership is special. We've found so many ways to enjoy these cars. We drive them. We tour in them. Race them. Wash them. Polish them. We show them at events all across America. Few cars have been so compelling. They draw owners together and make our lives more worthwhile. Quite an accomplishment for an automobile and for the men who have made them. We should be ever-thankful to Zora Arkus-Duntov, Dave McLellan, Dave Hill, and all the great engineers and designers past and present who have made it possible for so many people to love a car!

Where it all began, with a prototype poised on the turntable in the Grand Ballroom of New York's posh Waldorf Astoria Hotel, in January 1953. The Corvette was one of several GM Motorama "Dream Cars" that would go into production that year. Among others, the '53 Cadillac Eldorado, Oldsmobile Fiesta, and Buick Skylark.

Introduction

Our Sporting Ways

The Need for Faster, More Exhilarating Cars

"I feel the need. The need for speed!"

Tom Cruise may have made that line famous, but as a species we humans have felt that need for centuries. The automobile finally allowed us to bring that desire down to a personal level. Even before the turn of the century, gentlemen racers were testing their skills and the mettle of their motorcars in sporting contests. This need to compete is in our blood and in the automotive world it eventually came down to one all-encompassing idea: the sports car.

How one defines a sports car depends upon the era in which it was built. By modern standards the Chevrolet Corvette is a sports car, but in 1928 so was a Mercedes-Benz SSK, and in the 1930s a coachbuilt Delahaye 135M could be elegant enough to use for an evening out on the town yet rugged enough to compete in a local hill climb the next morning.

Americans had never been high on sports cars prior to the late forties. This was perhaps due to the fact that the idea was very European. Certainly there were sporting American cars—Cadillac, Packard, Lincoln, even Duesenberg offered speedsters—but they were nothing like the competition-bent designs of prewar Jaguars, ACs, and Alfa Romeos—smaller, agile and more powerful cars built for a purpose very few Americans could comprehend. Those who did purchased Bugattis, Alfa Romeos, Jaguars, and the like, and had them shipped home. They were few, however, and their sway on the American automotive industry was little felt. The American ideal of a sports car had yet to be realized.

The sports car, as we know it today, was really defined by racing. From the late 1930s, the shape of cars built for competition established the route automotive stylists would follow for decades. These were the cars that would influence Harley Earl's design for the Corvette.

The definition of a sports car changed from decade to decade. In the 1920s, a "sporting car" would have been an immense Mercedes-Benz SSK bodied with lightweight two-seat coachwork, such as this one-of-a-kind Boattail Speedster bodied in 1928 for an American owner by the Walter M. Murphy Company in Pasadena, California.

In the 1930s a coachbuilt Delahaye 135M could be elegant enough to use for an evening out on the town yet sporty enough to compete in a local hill climb the next morning.

The idea of a sporting car in the 1930s could have been anything from a Model A roadster to a mighty Model SJ Duesenberg, like this massive 154½-inch wheelbase Boattail Speedster bodied by Weymann.

It wasn't until the late 1940s that Americans began to experience firsthand the joys of driving small two-seaters like the MG TD. By 1952 there were 7,449 MGs registered in the United States and the MG had become the best selling imported sports car in America.

The little cars from Morris Garage had pried open the door. What drove through next was the Jaguar XK-120. Arbiters of American taste quickly declared it the *ne plus ultra* of sports cars and by 1952 there were 3,349 Americans enjoying the sheer pleasure of indulging themselves in Sir William Lyons' vision of what a sports car should be.

During this same period, New York auto importer Max Hoffman was introducing to America's automotive elite the 356 Porsche, while Luigi Chinetti's New York dealership had become the channel through which Enzo Ferrari's 166 and 212 models would pass into the hands of affluent American racing and sports car enthusiasts.

The success of these cars, however, was not sufficient enough to convince Detroit automakers that a market for such vehicles actually existed. In 1952, a total of 11,199 new sports cars were registered in America. This amounted to an insignificant 0.27 percent of car registrations for the year! If there was a sports car market in this country, it was exiguous at best, although it might have been better defined as a sports car movement that began in 1949. That was the year Ken Purdy wrote his most often quoted line in an article for *True* magazine titled "The Two-Seater Comes Back."

"Comes now a cloud on the horizon bigger than a man's hand which may portend a revival on this side of the water of the sports car—an automobile built for the sole purpose of going like a bat out of hell and never mind whether the girl friend likes it or not."

A narrow viewpoint perhaps but one shared by that handful of sports car enthusiasts who were buying Jaguars, MGs, Crosley Hotshots, and Kurtis-Kraft roadsters in the late forties.

The concept of the sports car as a small two-place roadster had its beginnings in Europe and reached a milestone in the late 1940s with models such as this trend-setting Ferrari 166MM Touring Barchetta.

In 1952, Porsche built a handful of small 356-based roadsters exclusively for the American market, the Porsche America. Imported by New York auto dealer Max Hoffman, the America and other Porsche 356 models helped convince U.S. automakers that there was indeed a market for such cars. (Owner John Paterek)

Considered one of the greatest influences on Harley Earl's design for the '53 Corvette, Sir William Lyons' stunning Jaguar XK-120 rewrote the book on postwar sports car design. Earl embraced many of the Jaguar's most sporting attributes in the Corvette's design, including the flowing fenderline, the absence of exterior embellishments, door handles, locks, and in true sports car form, a concealable folding top and the exclusion of roll-up side windows. Although most of these features made the Jaguar irresistible, they made the '53 Corvette unacceptable to all but the most avid of motoring enthusiasts.

Speaking before the Society of Automotive Engineers in 1953, Zora Arkus-Duntov said, "Considering the statistics, the American public does not want a sports car at all. But," he asked, "do the statistics give a true picture? As far as the American market is concerned," surmised Duntov, "it is still an unknown quantity, since an American sports car catering to American tastes, roads, way of living and national character has not yet been on the market." However, before the year was out, such a car would be on the market and the world according to Purdy would soon be populated with sporty two-seaters the likes of which Americans had never known.

MG was among the most prolific sports cars of all time and models like the MG TC, TD and TF played a fundamental role in introducing Americans to small two-place roadsters after World War II. (Cars courtesy Mike Goodman Sports Cars)

In England, the sports car was nothing new. Automakers like MG and Auto Carrier (AC) had been building them since the early thirties. Closely resembling the Jaguar SS-100, this AC ACE Sport Roadster, built in 1936, was typical of English two-seaters. (Owner David Campbell)

The first and perhaps most pure of sports cars to bear the Corvette name, models produced from 1953 to 1955 embodied the best characteristics of the MG, Jaguar, and Porsche. The model pictured is a 1955 V8 equipped model. The V8's were easily identified by the large "V" in CheVrolet. (Owner Lon Berger)

Dreams do come true. From Motorama Dream Car to Chevrolet production car was a quick step in 1953. Immediate demand for the car prompted the production of 300 Polo White cars bodied in Fiberglas. The public was so intrigued with the Fiberglas concept and the fledgling plastics industry so willing to help produce the car, that Chevrolet was persuaded to continue production in Fiberglas. The car pictured is an original, unrestored example owned by Chip Miller.

Chapter I

Dreams Do Come True

The Motorama Dream Car and
Corvettes of the Fifties

From Auto Show to automobile showroom was less of a step than most people think and a greater risk for General Motors than anyone at the time realized. The 1953 Corvette charted new waters for GM in the realm of automotive styling, captivating a car-hungry American public that was only just beginning to understand European sports car styling from the handful of MG TDs, Porsche 356s, and Jaguar XK-120s showing up on American roads.

The excitement surrounding the Corvette's public debut at the 1953 New York Motorama was due largely to its sleek, futuristic appearance and unique Fiberglas body. Initially, Chevrolet planned to build only 300 Corvettes out of Fiberglas and then switch to traditional steel bodies when tooling was readied. Before the final decision could be made, however, GM experienced something of an epiphany in plastic. The public was so intrigued with the Fiberglas concept and the fledgling plastics industry so willing to help produce the car, that Chevrolet was persuaded to continue production in Fiberglas. Building the bodies out of plastic set GM back $400,000, whereas manufacturing them in steel would have had a tooling cost estimated at $4.5 million!

Despite its low-slung, European stance and distinction as the nation's first production car with a Fiberglas body, the Corvette's design quickly drew criticism from consumers. Following the British theory for the construction of a sports roadster, the Corvette had no exterior door handles or door locks. Presumably one would only drive with the top raised in the foulest of weather, so why put locks on a car that would have its top down most of the time? There were no roll-up windows, either. Instead, Chevrolet used removable glass side curtains. The top itself was lightweight fabric and easily folded, innovatively stowed beneath a Fiberglas boot which added greatly to the dramatic lines of the car when the top was lowered.

An auspicious beginning. Crowds poured over the '53 Corvette at the GM Motorama. A proud Edward N. Cole, (behind the wheel) then Chevrolet's chief engineer and the driving force behind the car's development, and Chevrolet general manager Thomas Keating, at the Corvette's unveiling in January 1953. (Photo courtesy Automobile Quarterly, *1995)*

Early Corvettes come off the St. Louis assembly line. Here is the body drop on one of the first cars built in December, 1953. All but 300 of the 250,000 Corvettes built through November 7, 1969, were built in this plant as the first mass produced Fiberglas-bodied sports cars grew from a "Dream Car" to international auto celebrity. (Photo courtesy Automobile Quarterly, *1995)*

Still one of the best looking American cars of all time, the 1953 through 1955 Corvette was the epitome of classic sports car styling. (Owner Lon Berger).

The original Corvette body style was the closest Chevrolet ever came to creating an American sports car in the European idiom. Encompassing much of the contemporary styling seen on the Jaguar XK-120, the body lines were sleek and flowing, and in true roadster form the car had no exterior door handles or roll-up side windows. (Owner Lon Berger).

All of the aforementioned features made the first Corvette immediately popular with sports car cognoscenti, those who cared not for creature comforts but more for the essence of sports car design. And that was the greatest flaw in Chevrolet's planning.

Budget limitations required that Chevy engineers use an existing engine and transmission. Thus the '53-'54 Corvette was powered by a moderately "tweaked" overhead valve six-cylinder engine from the passenger car line, coupled to an automatic transmission. With a mere 150 horsepower and a torque converter two-speed, sports car enthusiasts who might have otherwise purchased as many cars as Chevrolet could build were anything but enthusiastic. The Corvette was intriguing to look at but less so to own.

Ford stylist Franklin Q. Hershey was quick to hone in on the Corvette's shortcomings and when the Thunderbird came to market in the fall of 1954, it had an easily operated convertible top, plus a removable hard top, a V8 engine, and roll-up windows. Ford called it a "Personal Luxury Car." Chevrolet called it trouble.

Historically, the road to progress is littered fender deep in ideas that didn't work, cars that after a few short years tumbled from lofty reverence as innovative concepts into the unclean shadows inhabited by motordom's also-rans. This was about to become the Corvette's fate. By late 1954, the car's

One of several concept cars based on the Corvette design theme, the Oldsmobile F88 toured America with the Motorama in 1954.

A short-lived competitor, the Ford Thunderbird was the only other production sports car built in America. T-Birds equipped with Supercharged engines, and known as "F" Birds, could have given the 'Vette some real head-to-head competition had Ford not discontinued the original two-passenger concept in 1958.

One of three Corvette-based Motorama Dream Cars shown in 1954, this version had a bolt-on hard top, which had Chevy put into production might have boosted early sales.

novelty was wearing thin. The 300 built in '53 had sold quickly but now nearly half of those produced for '54 were languishing on dealer lots. Harley Earl's dream car was about to become a nightmare. Enter Zora Arkus-Duntov.

A Belgian-born engineer of Russian ancestry, Duntov joined Chevrolet on May 1, 1953, and quickly began analyzing the problems which were curbing Corvette sales. On October 14, 1954, Duntov sent a confidential memorandum to Edward N. Cole, Chevrolet's chief engineer and Chevrolet engineer Maurice Olley. Wrote Duntov: "By the looks of it, the Corvette is on its way out. Dropping the car now will have an adverse effect internally and externally. It is admission of failure. Failure of aggressive thinking in the eyes of the organization, failure to develop a salable product in the eyes of the outside world." Duntov believed the Corvette's value had to be measured by its effect on the entire Chevrolet product line.

From the start, Duntov had been critical of the Corvette's high price, relative to its performance as a sports car. He felt that the Corvette did not have the value for the money. Concluded Duntov: "If the value of a car consists of practical values and emotional appeal, the sports car has very little of the first and consequently has to have an exaggerated amount of the second."

The early success of the Thunderbird had given Chevrolet even more reasons to revive the struggling Corvette. Duntov's concerns were that Ford's aggressive advertising would exploit a Chevrolet failure and since the Corvette was an important part of changing Chevrolet's family car image, canceling the project would have been an embarrassment for both Cole and GM.

As the '55 models were being readied for introduction, the idea of the Corvette being an embarrassment was something of a moot point. Chevrolet dealers were still sitting on 1,077 unsold '54s, amounting to nearly 30 percent of the previous year's production, and it was January 1955! For the new model year the assembly plant in St. Louis would add only 700 new models to dealer inventory.

If nothing else, Chevrolet answered one demand of would-be Corvette owners in '55 with the introduction of a V8 engine. There were actually two distinct models available, though most people think of the V8 simply as an engine option. To the contrary, the V8 was a separate car listed by a different stock number and base price. The Blue Flame Six was numbered 2934-6 and retailed for $2,774 while the V8 models were numbered 2934-8 and base-priced at $2,909. At a glance, both appeared to be the same, but upon closer inspection those with the V8 had an enlarged gold "V" in the name CheVrolet that appeared on the side of the car.

In 1955 Chevrolet answered one demand of would-be Corvette owners with the introduction of a V8 engine. The V8 was a separate model listed by a different stock number and with a different base price. The Blue Flame Six was model 2934-6 and retailed for $2,774 while the V8 models were numbered 2934-8 with a base price of $2,909.

With the introduction of a V8 model in 1955, Corvette was on the threshold of becoming a true high performance sports car. Exterior styling was virtually unchanged with the noted exception of the Chevrolet name on the front fenders, which had a large gold "V" to indicate a V8-equipped model.

Under the hood, the V8 with the Carter single four-barrel carburetor turned out 195 horsepower, 40 more than the Blue Flame offered in 1955. The extra horses turned the Corvette's mediocre 0–60 time of 11 seconds inside out at 8.7, according to *Road & Track's* July 1955 road test. Quarter-mile time improved from 18 seconds to 16.5, and top speed increased from 107.1 mph to 119.1 mph. Despite the improvement in performance, reported *R&T*, the new V8 low friction engine yielded 2 to 3 miles per gallon more than had the 150 hp six.

As was the case with the Blue Flame six, the new V8 was also a passenger car engine that had been modified, this time equipped with the Carter four-barrel "power pack" carburetor and a special camshaft which alone accounted for 15 of the extra horses. The V8 displaced 265 cubic inches with a 3.75 in x 3.0 in bore x stroke, and an 8:1 compression ratio.

For 1955, Chevrolet offered a Corvette with a V8 under the hood. With the Carter single four-barrel carburetor, the V8 turned out 195 horsepower, 40 more than the Blue Flame offered in 1955. The extra horses turned the Corvette's mediocre 0-60 time of 11 seconds inside out at 8.7, according to Road & Track's *July 1955 road test. Quarter-mile time improved from 18 seconds to 16.5, and top speed increased from 107.1 mph to 119.1 mph. The optional V8 was ordered on 3,080 of the 3,467 Corvettes produced in 1956.*

Even with the larger engine, the Corvette failed to get high marks from the automotive press. *Road & Track* remarked after a 1,450-mile road test that "the V8 gives startling performance, as might well be expected, but the transmission and brake deficiencies still will not satisfy the demands of either competitor or of the true sports car enthusiast." Test reports throughout the year showed the Corvette's brakes as "more than adequate for ordinary usage." Of course, *ordinary* was not in the sports car enthusiast's vocabulary.

More troublesome than poor brakes was the Corvette's transmission—in retrospect, a bad choice on Chevrolet's part. Though many buyers were satisfied with the 2-speed Powerglide automatic gearbox neatly positioned on the floor and looking for all the world like a manual stick shift, many would have preferred more than looks. A 3-speed manual was added as an option late in 1955 but it was too little, too late. Ford had been wise enough to see Chevrolet's error and offered both automatic and manual transmissions in 1955; one of several reasons why the early Thunderbirds were more successful. Still, the Corvette was more of a sports car in the Jaguar tradition. It had the British look tempered with American taste, yet offered drivers a real sports car treatment. The Corvette would never be called a "Personal Luxury Car," nor would Chevrolet ever abandon the two-seater format, as would Ford after 1957.

With the introduction of the V8, Corvette was on the threshold of becoming a true high performance sports car and what the following years were to bring under the guidance of Ed Cole, Maurice Olly and Zora Arkus-Duntov, would write a new chapter in American automotive history.

With planning under way for an all-new Corvette to debut in 1956, Harley Earl's team of gifted stylists made substantial changes to the Corvette body. Every aspect of the original design was altered and refined. "All the designers were enamored by the Mercedes-Benz 300SL Gullwing coupe," recalls Bob Cadaret, who worked as a stylist on the Chevy design staff. "From the windshield forward, the 300SL was the predominant influence on the styling of the 1956 Corvette."

Another principal influence on the 1956 Corvette body came from the LaSalle II roadster, a 1955 GM Motorama car. The LaSalle had coved insets on the front fenders that curved well into the doors and were painted a contrasting color to accent their shape. Another variation of this sculptured, concave effect was also shown on the '55 Chevrolet Biscayne concept car, which had the cove turned in the opposite direction. The Corvette's new fender styling evolved directly from the Motorama cars.

By February 1955, the basic design of the 1956 Corvette was completed. This time GM had gone to school at Ford's expense adapting the best features of the Thunderbird. The new Corvette would have roll-up windows, with available power assist, exterior door handles, an improved convertible top mechanism, also with an available power assist, and a new extra-cost auxiliary hardtop.

With the '56 models, output from the V8 was increased to 210 hp, with 225 hp available through an optional dual four-barrel carburetor. The V8 engine significantly improved the Corvette's overall weight distribution, being

In the middle of the instrument cluster on '53-'55 models was the tachometer (including a lap counter in the form of an odometer that actually kept track of the number of revolutions the engine made). Note the manual-looking automatic stick shift. A real manual gearbox was not available on Corvettes until very late in 1955 and only around two dozen were ordered that way.

By 1957 Corvettes were finding their way into motorsports competition. At Sebring in 1957, Dr. Dick Thompson, driving car number 4 won the GT Class. (Photos courtesy Automobile Quarterly, *1995)*

"All the designers were enamored by the Mercedes-Benz 300SL Gullwing coupe," recalls Bob Cadaret, who worked as a stylist on the Chevy design staff. "From the windshield forward, the 300SL was the predominant influence on the styling of the 1956 Corvette."

A principal influence on the design of the new 1956 Corvette was the LaSalle II roadster, a 1955 GM Motorama Dream Car. The LaSalle had coved insets on the front fenders that curved well into the doors and painted a contrasting color to accent their shape.

One of the most popular factory options in 1956 was the removable hardtop, no charge in exchange for the soft top or an additional $215.20 if the buyer wanted both.

some 40 pounds lighter than its six-cylinder predecessor. Changes beneath the hood also demanded commensurate modifications to the suspension in order to take full advantage of the added power.

Duntov's reaction to the handling characteristics of his V8-equipped 1955 prototype were mixed at best, and he proposed a number of engineering revisions. "The target," he explained in *Auto Age,* "was to attain such handling characteristics that the driver of some ability could get really high performance safely." Duntov felt this objective could be met through suspension changes that focused on increased high-speed stability, consistent steering wheel response over a wide range of conditions, and improved power transmission to the rear wheels on turns.

With the standard synchromesh three-speed manual transmission, the Corvette emerged as a true driver's automobile in 1956. "In almost every respect, the 1956 Corvette is a very satisfying car on the highway," wrote *Sports Cars Illustrated,* "and supplements astonishing performance with a high level of road-holding."

Windows in the door were new for 1956. Power option was rare and added $64.60 to the price of the car. Only 547 Corvettes were equipped with this feature.

New body styling for 1956 is still among the most beautiful in Corvette history. The sleek lines of the rear fenders integrated taillights, bumpers, and exhaust tips into one grand sweep.

Red on red, the '56 interior is superbly accented by the contrasting white instrument panel and door trim.

The transistorized, signal-seeking radio was a new feature in 1956, adding a hefty $198.90 to the price of the car. The most expensive option available, it cost more than the 240 hp engine upgrade and Powerglide transmission!

With the '56 models, output from the V8 was increased to 210 hp, with 225 hp and 240 hp upgrades available. The V8 engine significantly improved the Corvette's overall weight distribution, being some 40 pounds lighter than its six-cylinder predecessor. Changes beneath the hood also demanded commensurate modifications to the suspension in order to take full advantage of the added power.

41

For its 1956 models Chevrolet had gone to school at Ford's expense adapting the best features of the Thunderbird. The new Corvette had roll-up windows, with available power assist, exterior door handles, an improved convertible top mechanism, also with an available power assist, and a new extra-cost auxiliary hardtop. (Owner Jerry Palmer).

Breaking from the previous year's limited color schemes, Corvettes could now be ordered in any of eight exterior colors: Onyx Black, Polo White, Cascade Green, Aztec Copper, Arctic Blue, Venetian Red, Shoreline Beige, and Silver. For an additional $19, the RPO 440 option gave owners a choice of beige or silver painted coves to contrast the body color.

Also among the list of firsts for '56 were dealer installed seatbelts, an adjustable passenger seat, and a transistorized signal-seeking radio. In all, Corvette production jumped from 700 in '55 to a respectable 3,467 in '56. Sales figures for the year gave Chevrolet marketing managers a good idea of what appealed most to Corvette buyers. Of the total number of cars sold, only 276 were purchased with the base engine. For an additional $172, more than 3,000 were ordered with the optional 225 hp V8; 1,510 coupled to the manual gearbox and 1,570 teamed with Powerglide. The hardtop was among the most popular of all options, ordered on 2,076 cars; 629 in place of the soft top and 1,447 as a $215.20 addition.

For bench racers, here's a little bit of 'Vette trivia guaranteed to win a steak dinner. Through April of '56, all convertible tops were power operated. With the availability of a manual top in May, the hydraulic assist became a $107.60 option. A total of 2,682 were produced with power tops and buyers had a choice of white, beige, or black fabric. Just for the record only 103 people opted for black, 1,840 purchased white and 895, beige. The Venetian Red 1956 model pictured is a rare example equipped with power windows, heater delete option, the 265 cid 225 hp V8 with solid lifters, automatic transmission, and 3.55:1 rear axle ratio. What makes it even rarer is the fact that it is an original car with only 24,000 miles!

Owner Jerry Palmer, of Fountain Valley, California, has researched his car down to the nth degree. It was the 2,790th car manufactured at the St. Louis plant and was built in May of '56. As equipped, the base price was $3,120 plus $198.90 for the radio, $188.50 for the Powerglide, $64.60 for power windows, $172.20 for the 225 hp engine, $5.40 for parking brake alarm, $8.65 for courtesy lights, and $32.50 for whitewall tires. To preserve the original steering wheel, Palmer wrapped it with a red leather steering wheel cover. "It's not authentic," says Palmer, "but what's underneath it is!"

With the introduction of the completely restyled 1956 model line, Cole, Earl, and Duntov had in one bold stroke redeemed the Corvette. The '56 models were a hallmark in the evolution of the breed, the first real American sports car, cars that arrived at the momentous crossroad, and made the right turn.

In 1958 the Corvette was extensively restyled and dual headlamps with separate high- and low-beam lamps were at the head of the list. The following year, very little changed on the outside, with the exception of chrome trim on the trunk lid which was deleted along with the hood ridges introduced in '58.

Marking the end of the solid axle models, the '62s have often been declared the last Corvettes true to the spirit of the original. Perhaps this is so for collectors who appreciate the flawless balance of the roadster body, the sweet curves of the fender coves and the sheer simplicity of the car's design. The Corvette would never again appear so unpretentious. The '62 models truly marked the end of an era. (Photos by Dennis Adler)

Chapter 2

Form Pairs with Function

The Cars of the Sixties

In 1961 the first major styling changes in several years were introduced: the first use of round taillight lenses and a new tapered look to the rear which would forecast the look of the next generation Sting Ray. In 1962, the Corvette reached what many call its high water mark with the introduction of the 327 small block.

To many die-hard Corvette enthusiasts, the 1962 models are considered the last true Corvettes made. Others believe the end came in 1967. Personally, we're of the belief that the 'Vette bought the farm after 1971, when the big horsepower 454 engines were emasculated by Federal regulations. As to the exact moment the music stopped, it's all a matter of conjecture: '62, '67, or '71. It stopped. And did not return until the late 1980s.

In 1962, with Daytona and two SCCA class titles under its belt, the Corvette was in the second year of a two-year transition in body styling, which was to segue into the third-generation 'Vette and the famed 1963 Sting Ray Coupe.

Although similar to the 1958-'60 models, the '61 Corvettes offered a brand-new rear quarter appearance with freshened fender styling, featuring a raised speed-line crease that kicked up just forward of the rear wheel arch and then tapered back into a new tail section, accented by four recessed taillights. Tailpipes would no longer exit through the rear bumpers as in the past. The exhaust note would now play through conventional pipes exiting beneath the brightwork.

As for incidentals, a new grille shape was introduced and the formerly chromed headlight bezels were now painted body color. This year would also mark the last year that the Corvette could be ordered with the coves painted in a contrasting color.

The '62 model year was distinguished by several important firsts. These would be the first Corvettes to use narrow whitewall tires; chromed rocker panels were introduced (some feel it was a test to see if the public would accept the design, as it was already slated for the '63 Sting Ray); and a new fin treatment highlighted a change to the 'Vette's cove design.

Aside from some minor changes, all of the big news for '62 was under the Corvette's hood. This was the year Chevrolet introduced the 327 cubic inch small block V8, with

Styling had changed little since 1958 and only minor trim distinguished the first Corvette of the sixties. Under the hood, cast aluminum cylinder heads were added to the power arsenal. An optional 315 hp, 283 cid V8 was offered with a manual transmission, and an aluminum radiator was available for the first time, offered with high-lift cam-equipped engines.

horsepower ratings from 250 to 360. (It has turned out to be the most popular V8 engine ever produced by Detroit.) The old fuel-injected 315 hp, 283 V8 was discontinued as were dual four-barrel carbs, which had been a Corvette standard since 1956. The base engine for '62 was a 250 hp motor. All '62 engines used a tach drive, whereas in the past only solid lifter, fuel-injected engines had this feature. For 1962, the 360 hp rated V8 was the only engine offered with fuel injection, which was duly noted by a badge on the front fenders. The 340 hp engines drew their fuel through a new single large AFB carburetor. Both of the hi-po engines were equipped with seven-fin cast alloy valve covers, while the 250 and 300 hp engines had painted, stamped steel valve covers. And all of the engines came with decals denoting their horsepower ratings.

    With an exhaust note resonant as that of Shelby's Ford-powered Cobras hanging in the air, whether one chose

The rear deck styling introduced in 1961 was a precursor of the '63 Corvette's new taillight and fender design.

The '62 model year will be best remembered as the first for the 327 "small block" V8, the most successful engine in Chevrolet history. The optional fuel-injected 327 delivered 360 hp.

the Powerglide automatic or the slick-looking four speed-gear box, at full throttle the '62 Corvettes could knock you back in your seat!

Among the lasts attributed to the '62 Corvette, it marked the final year for the solid axle, exposed highlights, and an opening trunk.

Was the '62 really the last great Corvette? Well, one would have to ponder that question in light of both the popularity and value today of the '63 Split Window Coupes, and the rarefied '69 'Vettes equipped with the ZL-1 optioned 500 hp 427 cid engines. Back in '69, the engine option alone was a $3,000 bump over base price! One thing is for certain through, the styling of the '56-'62 Corvettes has never been surpassed for pure sports car appeal. And if looks alone could kill, the '61 and '62 Corvettes were definitely deadly!

A purely functional cockpit, the dashboard of late fifties and early sixties models left little to be desired. The tachometer was placed right below the speedometer and center on the steering wheel, the gear shift located to fall right at the driver's hand.

Arguably the greatest Corvette of all time, the 1962 model marked the end of the solid axle era, exposed headlights and trunks. It was perhaps the most gracefully designed Corvette of the sixties. (Owner Bruce Meyer).

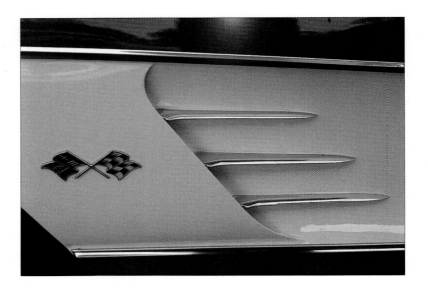

Images can define a car as much as a name. The sculptured Corvette side cove introduced in 1956 and used as a styling feature through 1962 is one of the single most identifiable design elements in automotive history.

Chevrolet departed from the European styling that had guided Corvette design since 1953. The 1963 Corvette Sting Ray rewrote the book from the four wheel independent suspension up. The new Bill Mitchell-inspired design featured streamlined styling, concealed head lamps and for the first time two distinct models, convertible and coupe.

It's interesting how three little words, "Split Window Coupe" describe the '63 Corvette without any further embellishment. It is one of the few cars in all of automotive history that can be brought to mind without even saying the year, or even the make. It can only be a '63 Corvette.

When the Sting Ray was introduced it was as if Chevrolet had reinvented the Corvette. Engines were completely revamped from the cooling system to the Rochester fuel-injection system—the first major overhaul of the design of the injector system since its introduction in 1957.

The Sting Ray's new engine delivered 360 hp and delivered it posthaste, burying the tach through every gear— zero to sixty in 5.6 seconds, flying through the quarter mile in 14.2 at 102 mph, and reaching a terminal velocity of 151 mph. Wrote *Road & Track* after testing an early production model with the 360 hp engine and 3.70:1 final drive, "As a purely sporting car, the new Corvette will know few peers on road or track. It has proved, in its 'stone-age form,' the master of most production line competitors; in its nice, shiny new concept it ought to be nearly unbeatable." *Car and Driver* declared the Sting Ray ". . .second to no other production car in road-holding and still the most powerful."

The '63 Corvettes brought many new owners into the Chevy fold. Sales for 1963 came in at an almost even split between the Sting Ray Coupe at 10,594 cars and the new Sting Ray Roadster selling just a handful more at 10,919 cars.

The biggest criticism Chevrolet suffered was over the Sting Ray Coupe's split window. In *Corvette: America's Star Spangled Sports Car,* author Karl Ludvigsen cataloged the Split Window's litany of editorial barbs:

Road & Track: "our only complaint about the interior was in the coupe, where all we could see in the rear view mirror was that silly bar splitting the rear window down the middle."

Car Life: "The bar down the center of the rear window makes it all but impossible to see out via the rear view mirror."

Motor Trend: "The rear window on the coupe is designed more for looks than practicality, and any decent view to the rear will have to be through an exterior side-view mirror."

Car and Driver: "Luggage space is surprisingly roomy but central window partition ruins rear view."

And from Europe, *Autocar* remarked: "Nothing can be seen of the tail through the divided rear window, which makes reversing in confined quarters rather precarious."

Reinventing the Corvette for 1963, GM design chief Bill Mitchell created a uniquely American sports car that set itself apart from European contemporaries. (Owner Chip Miller)

The most controversial feature of the '63 Corvette was the split rear window, a design which has set this single model apart from all others and given it the unique distinction of being described with just three words, Split Window Coupe.

The '63 Corvette introduced a new idea, concealed headlights. Designed into the body contours the headlight housing rolled over 180 degrees to expose the headlamps.

It has been said that the split window was inspired by GM design chief Bill Mitchell, despite the fact that Duntov was against it. If the split window was a battle of wills, Duntov prevailed. In '64 it was gone! This also led to some good natured, but deeply felt, kidding among performance enthusiasts. "The 'sting' had been removed from the Sting Ray," was a saying that Cobra fans used a great deal, but their chiding was unrequited.

The '64 Corvette was indeed a better car. Extensive work had been done to improve the ride characteristics, lessening the harshness owners of '63s experienced from the new four-wheel independent suspension. Improved insulation, stiffer body panels, and a redesigned muffler system also helped quiet things on the inside. As for performance, horsepower ratings reached an all-time high for the 327 cubic inch small-block, achieving 375 hp with fuel injection. A potent combination, Sting Ray and 375 fuel injected horses; more than 1 horsepower per cubic inch of displacement!

The '64s were available with a lengthy inventory of options. There were aluminum cast wheels, a 36.5 gallon fuel tank, heavy-duty brakes, performance suspension, Positraction, and of course, the 375 horsepower Ramjet fuel-injected V8 and 4-speed transmission.

In competition, the '64s ran up an impressive record, winning the GT class at 12 Hours of Sebring; the GT class at Daytona Continental; and the SCCA B Production National Championship.

Among the more desirable early Corvettes, the '64 falls short of the '63 and '65 models in popularity. As history has proven, '64 was a transition year. In '63 the Sting Ray was introduced with all of its innovations, which created a large "stir" in the performance world. In '64, the car was being refined. The '65 models would introduce four-wheel disc brakes and the 396 cid/425 hp "big block," launching Corvette into the Muscle Car era. It's ironic, but when Chevrolet did away with Mitchell's divided rear window, they unintentionally created a styling anomaly that would forever distinguish the '63 Corvette. For what it's worth, Chevrolet sold 10,594 Coupes in '63, while only 8,304 were purchased in '64.

The 1960s would mark the greatest evolution of the Corvette since its introduction.

The Sting Ray cockpit was a sight to behold. One look through the door on the dealer showroom floor and most people were already sold.

Solving the problem of placing a radio in a narrow center console was solved by simply mounting it sideways!

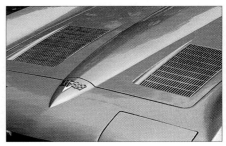

Clean lines of the '63 Corvette nose and hood were distinctive styling traits penned by Mitchell for the Sting Ray concept race car and refined by Mitchell and his staff for the XP-700 prototype coupe in 1959. The lines for the new Corvette model were already finalized by April 1960, including the split rear window, which almost split the relationship between Mitchell and Zora Arkus-Duntov. Duntov wanted better rear visibility and Mitchell stated flatly, "If you take that off you might as well forget the whole thing."

One of the hallmarks of the sixties was the introduction of the L-88 option in 1967. Although not to be sold to the general public the L-88 option found great acceptance among those who spent their weekends at Willow Springs, Riverside, Watkins Glen, and countless venues across the country, where the sounds of open exhausts and screaming tires were welcomed. The L-88 was the 427 with all the stops pulled out. Based on the stock 427 cid Mark IV engine, the L-88 had aluminum cylinder heads, full-race cam, an 850-cfm Holley four-barrel carburetor atop an aluminum manifold, no smog equipment, and a compression ratio of 12.5:1. In 1967 only 20 L-88 optioned cars were produced, cars that could do 13-second quarter miles and deliver 560 hp.

Duntov had been against the Corvette's rear window design in '63. If the split window was a battle of wills between Mitchell and Duntov, Zora prevailed. The '64 Corvette was indeed a better car, not only for rearward visibility but mechanically. Extensive work had been done to improve the ride characteristics, lessening the harshness owners of '63s experienced from the new four-wheel independent suspension. Improved insulation, stiffer body panels and a redesigned muffler system also helped quiet things on the inside. As for performance, horsepower ratings reached an all-time high for the 327 cubic inch small-block, achieving 375 hp with fuel injection; no less than 1.5 horsepower per cubic inch of displacement.

The 1964 Sting Ray coupe was burdened with being an interim model while changes in the design and engineering of the car were being made. In '65 four wheel disc brakes were introduced making the '64 an orphan model among Corvette collectors today. This remarkable example of the '64 model is completely original, right down to the paint, and has clocked only 24,431 miles!

The 327 cid V8 could be ordered with the L-76 option giving 365 hp. One step up was the L-84 with fuel-injection and 10 additional horses. A total of 7,171 cars were ordered with the L-76 motor and 1325 with the L-84 option.

The '64 Corvette was one of the most stylishly appointed high-performance sports cars in the world. European automotive journalist and race driver Paul Frere wrote in Auto, Motor und Sport, *"If there were people who doubted whether or not large American companies knew how to build a real sports car or whether or not they were interested in building one, they all know differently now."*

Roadsters still outsold coupes almost 2 to 1 in the early sixties. Considered one of the best model years ever, 1965 Sting Rays introduced four wheel disc brakes and mid-year the Mark IV 396 cid "big block" V8. Outside exhaust pipes (below the rocker panels) are another new addition that give the Corvette an even more aggressive look.

With the all-new styling introduced in '68, the L-88 option managed to find its way into four times as many cars as the previous year, but the new Corvette was not the car it had been from 1963 to 1967. For many Corvette cognoscenti, this was the year the car lost its magic. For others, it was the beginning of a new romance. Either way, the fifth generation 'Vette was something altogether different from past designs.

Much of the car's new styling evolved from Bill Mitchell's 1965 Mako Shark II concept car. More than a visual tease for auto shows in '65, it was actually a trial balloon to test public reaction to the Corvette's proposed new shape. For all intents, however, the '68 design was already committed. The Mako Shark II was an exaggerated, pizzazzed version of what Mitchell had already proposed as a replacement for the aging Corvette Sting Ray introduced in '63. Histori-

Corvette bid farewell to the 1960s with one of the most powerful engine options ever, the L-88, providing 430 hp from the "big block" Mark IV 427 cid V8. Only 116 Corvettes were so equipped in 1969. (Owner Chip Miller)

Performance enthusiasts found the 1969 L-88 optioned Corvette simply irresistible. The engine option called for an increase in price of $1,032.15. Only 116 were ordered.

cally, it has become one of the most controversial models in the Corvette saga.

The '68 model was the first Corvette to receive mixed reviews since the early fifties, and in almost every instance the criticism was directed at the car's styling.

"If there's such a thing as a psychedelic car, the 1968 Corvette is it," said *Road & Track*. The magazine concluded its initial review by saying, "We wish we could express more enthusiasm for the new model but we feel that the general direction of the changes is away from Sports Car and toward Image and Gadget Car." Other magazines were less charitable!

Car and Driver ripped its '68 test car from bumper to bumper, berating everything from the ash tray to the T-top and finally declared it "unfit to road test."

In 1966 Chevy bumped the "big block" to 427 cubic inches and 425 hp, making the '65s unique as the only year with a 396 cid V8. The '66 models were pretty much carryover designs in most respects and sales hit an all time high of 17,762 convertibles and 9,958 coupes.

One fully stuffed engine room. Under the hood of an L-88 optioned Corvette there was little space not occupied by the "big block" 427 cid, 430 hp V8.

No room for error in fueling the L-88 either. Factory warning on center console reminded owners that 103 research octane and 95 motor octane were the minimum fuel requirements.

Although the '68 model was arguably the worst car in the Corvette's history, you couldn't have proven it by public response. In deference to the opinions of the motoring press, Americans flocked to their Chevy dealers making 1968 the best sales year ever to that time, with 9,936 coupes and 18,630 convertibles being sold.

You might consider 1968 a shaking out year for the new Corvette which was somewhat rushed to market and at that was a year later than had been originally planned. There had been a one-year hiatus for the Sting Ray name which was readopted in '69, although now spelled *Stingray*. Duntov and the Chevrolet engineering department had spent most of '68 making quick fixes to problems noted by the press and owners alike. The '69 model was better, although not by much and it didn't really seem to matter since sales continued to increase. For the first time ever, more coupes sold than convertibles, 22,129 to 16,633—a turning point in consumer tastes, which went unrecognized at the time. Within five years, the convertible would be dead. Well, not dead, let's just say dormant.

In 1969 Corvette established several new milestones, including the introduction of the 350 cid small-block (replacing the 327) and the limited offering of the ultimate production car motor, the ZL-1 competition engine, displacing 427

The Mako Shark II was Bill Mitchell's personal project. In 1965 and '66, when the concept car made the international show circuit, it became one of the most talked about and criticized designs in the world. Everyone from Car Life to Hot Rod in America and Motor and Autocar in Europe had something to say about the Mako Shark II. Most of it was less than charitable. What no one knew was that they were looking at the general outline of the Sting Ray's successor. Mitchell and stylist Larry Shinoda had created a flashy show car packed with innovative ideas, but moreover, they had given the world a preview of things to come.

cubic inches and developing anywhere from 500 hp to 600 hp, depending upon whose dyno you believed. The official Corvette option book described it as the ZL-1 Optional Special 427 CI Engine, with a list price of $3,000. That was three grand over the base price of a new Corvette, which in 1969 started at $4,780.95 for a Stingray coupe.

For performance car enthusiasts, '69 could be considered the beginning of the end, as Federally-mandated emissions controls began to take effect. The 1970s would become the decade of low performance, with muscle cars being replaced by economy cars, the Middle East oil embargo beginning an ever spiraling upward increase in the price of a gallon of gasoline, and a major shift in American consumer buying trends. The seventies changed our priorities; for the first time since the Corvette was introduced, miles per gallon would mean more to buyers than miles per hour. The Corvette would endure but the road leading to the next high-performance era in American automotive history would be a long and costly one.

One year after the new model was introduced, Chevy resurrected the Sting Ray name for Corvette, only now it was one word added in script above the fender louvers. Despite the cold welcome the car had received from automotive magazines, buyers were warmly accepting the car in record numbers. In 1969 more than 38,000 new Corvettes were sold. The customers had proven Mitchell and Shinoda correct. A milestone was reached on November 19, 1969, when the 250,000th Corvette, a gold convertible, rolled off the St. Louis production line.

From Mako Shark II to 1968 Corvette was a big step for Chevrolet. They had once again reinvented the Corvette, only this time the new model was not met with rave reviews. It had been rushed to market, was fraught with pro-duction problems and a design that perhaps was not altogether practical. The '68 model was sharply criticized by the American press and Car and Driver *declared it "unfit to road test."*

*Not all of the Corvette's glory faded after 1971. BFGoodrich, the American
radial company, took the BFG-sponsored John Greenwood Corvette to
LeMans in 1972 where it ran at sustained speeds of over 200 mph.*

Chapter 3

Building an Image

The Great Racers

"Even if the vast majority of sports car buyers do not intend to race them and most likely will never drive flat out, the potential performance of the car is of primordial value to its owner."
—Zora Arkus-Duntov

Although the 1956 Corvette offered a potent combination of V8 power and performance handling, Corvette was without credentials on the race track. Duntov knew that a legacy of racing successes, like those of Jaguar, Porsche, and MG, was necessary to ensure the Corvette's long-term survival. When asked just how important racing was to the Corvette, Duntov recalls, "Very important."

Intimately familiar with European sports cars, Duntov had a unique perspective on the history, development, and demographics of these cars and their buyers. During the fall of 1953, he addressed a group of automotive engineers on the subject. "All commercially successful sports cars were promoted by participation in racing with specialized or modified cars," stressed Duntov. "Even if the vast majority of sports car buyers do not intend to race them and most likely will never drive flat out, the potential performance of the car is of primordial value to its owner."

Corvettes had been in competition since Chevrolet first put a V8 under the hood in 1955. That year Chevrolet set the stock car record for the Pike's Peak Hill Climb, and every year since, Corvettes have won in either SCCA, Showroom Stock, or vintage competition.

A champion in motorsports competition, Corvettes compiled a remarkable record of victories between 1956 and 1971: SCCA C-Production Champion in '56; first in class at Sebring, SCCA B-Production Champion and B-Sports/Racing Champion in 1957; first in GT at Sebring in '58 and SCCA B-Production Champion from 1958 to 1965! In 1960, Chevy racked up another first in class at Sebring, the SCCA C-Sports/Racing Championship, and an impressive eighth overall finish at Le Mans! In '61, the 'Vette's trophy shelf added another first at Sebring and in the Pikes Peak hill climb. The following year, Corvettes claimed all the checkered flags in SCCA A-Production and a first in class at the Daytona Continental.

The PPE was painted an almost blinding shade of purple and contrasted by white coves, bright chromed wheels and roll bar and the indiscreet absence of a conventional windshield.

Through 1971, Chevy continued to dominate with a string of stunning finishes at Daytona, Sebring, and in SCCA competitions. Even in its declining years, throughout the late seventies and early eighties, the Corvette managed to show some backbone in SCCA events, not to mention the marque's success in Showroom Stock competition.

Of course, every Corvette had the potential to be a race car, but there are some examples that have become legendary. Just as the Corvette was hitting its stride, the Automobile Manufacturers Association (AMA) adopted a resolution in June 1957 that required members to end all performance-oriented advertising and sponsorship of competition

The 1959 Corvette Purple People Eater Mk III was the last of a color classed lineage that began in 1957 with Chicago's Nickey Chevrolet, and a deep purple Corvette SR-2 race car. With Nickey Chevrolet's sponsorship, driver Jim Jeffords won two consecutive SCCA B Production championships, first in a '58 Corvette dubbed the Purple People Eater Mk II, and the following year in this car, a new '59 model, the PPE Mk III.

The '59 'Vette wore the number 1 in competition, noting the previous year's championship. The PPE was a stock '59 stripped down for racing—as so many were in the late fifties because Corvettes were about the most affordable street car you could "hot up" for competition.

For competition, Jeffords routed a straight exhaust system from the 283 small-block through the passenger's side rocker panel with two pipes coming through just below the door.

events, including technical assistance. Many speculated that the AMA ban was a relief for Detroit automakers, since the battle for horsepower was costing them millions of dollars. Ultimately, factory-supported competition efforts continued; they simply shifted from open to covert operations. "Racing was the thing that actually saved the Corvette," remarked Carroll Shelby, the designer of the car's number one competitor.

Despite the loss of official support, Corvettes continued to be raced after the AMA doctrine was signed by GM. One of the most famous was a car, well actually a series of cars, with the unlikely name of Purple People Eater.

You could call the 1959 Corvette Purple People Eater Mk III an iteration of an iteration, last of a color classed lineage that began in 1957 with Chicago's Nickey Chevrolet, and a deep purple Corvette SR-2 race car.

With Nickey Chevrolet's sponsorship, driver Jim Jeffords won two consecutive SCCA B Production championships, first in a '58 Corvette dubbed the Purple People Eater Mk II, and the following year in a new '59 model, the PPE Mk III. The new car wore the number 1 in competition, noting the previous year's championship.

Under the hood of the PPE was a 290 hp, 282 cid Ramjet fuel-injected V8.

The PPE was a stock '59 'Vette stripped down for racing—as so many were in the late fifties because Corvettes were about the most affordable street car you could "hot up" for competition. The car was painted an almost blinding shade of purple and contrasted by white coves, bright chromed wheels and roll bar and the indiscreet absence of a conventional windshield. Under the hood, locked tight with a guaranteed-to-psyche-out-the-competition turnbuckle heavy enough to latch the door on a Freightliner, was a 290 hp, 283 cu. in. Ramjet fuel-injected small-block V8.

For competition, Jeffords cut down roughly the top third of the windshield and cut the A-pillar and door post to match. He also routed the exhaust naturally without mufflers, through the passenger's side rocker panel just behind the door.

As Corvettes in competition go, the PPE was a great car in the straights with plenty of acceleration. In the corners, 'Vettes tended to give up a little to their competitors, and their brakes were none too spectacular either, as everyone within Chevrolet, including Duntov and Cole realized. Still, a driver with Jeffords' skills could manhandle the 'Vette and outdrive better and faster cars. On the plus side, Corvettes seldom broke.

After the back-to-back SCCA titles, the PPE Mk III was put up for sale and came into the hands of racer Bob Spooner who campaigned the car as number 33 in the '61

The driver-side Plexiglas windscreen was an on-again, off-again feature of the PPE. Originally, Jeffords cut down roughly the top third of the windshield and cut the A-pillars and door posts to match. Later in the season he jettisoned the full-width windshield for a pillarless curved windscreen on the driver's side. Second owner Bob Spooner went to a full Plexiglas windscreen, and when Miller found it the second Jeffords configuration was back in place.

SCCA season. With a fresh coat of purple and a new full width Plexiglas windscreen, (Jeffords had gone from this design to a pillarless curved windscreen on the driver's side in mid-'59), Spooner took the Nickey car into wheel-to-wheel combat. "We left a lot of fiberglass on the track [that season]" says Spooner, who was not above full body contact in competition. "In 1962 we ran the national circuit, racing all over, including Cumberland, Maryland, Marlboro Raceway in Virginia, plus the rest of the regular tracks," recalls Spooner. He finished the '62 season second in national points to Don Yenko. Not a bad ending for a race car that was already once retired. Spooner sold the PPE Mk III in 1963, and in proper fashion, as most old race cars do, it faded into obscurity having served its owners well.

When it comes to race cars, there is an old aphorism worth remembering, that race cars are a lot like weeds: unless you destroy them completely, they have a tendency to keep coming back. The Purple People Eater MK III is a perfect example. The car lay dormant until 1974, when current owner Chip Miller purchased it in "original" condition, totally unaware of the car's competition history or former owners. "It was in pretty rough shape," recalls Miller, "but I just felt that there was something special about the car."

Still in running condition, it fired up with one turn of the key emitting an ear-splitting, deep-throated *b-a-r-a-a-p!* With a little cleanup and a set of 8-inch Rally wheels and race tires, Miller took the battle-scared '59 'Vette into autocrosses with NCCC for an entire year before the engine failed and it was rolled into friend Ken Heckert's shop for an eventual repair and restoration. It spent the next decade under a tarp in Heckert's paint shop serving as a table.

It was during research for the restoration that Miller and Heckert discovered the identity of the car as the very same Corvette in which Jim Jeffords had won his second SCCA championship. In 1985, Heckert happened across a picture of a car in Karl Ludvigsen's book *Corvette—America's Star-Spangled Sports Car* that looked a lot like the old '59 'Vette. It had a similar style Plexiglas windscreen and the number 33 painted on the side. Ludvigsen's office could offer no further details on the car, and at the time it seemed they had come to a dead end. The car remained a table for another two years. Then in 1987, Miller met Mike Pillsbury. An expert on Corvette race cars, Pillsbury was able to identify the car and its driver, Bob Spooner. Both Miller and Heckert were now convinced that they had unknowingly purchased the car driven in 1961 and 1962 by Spooner, the very same 1959 Corvette in which Jim Jeffords had won his second SCCA championship.

After corresponding with Spooner and finally interviewing him on the phone, Miller was able to confirm that the car was indeed the Nickey/Jeffords Purple People Eater Mk III. A trip to St. Louis to see Spooner in the summer of 1989 netted hours of interview tape, pictures, and records. The weed was about to sprout once again.

After four years in restoration at Heckert's shop and countless hours of documenting the authenticity of every detail of the restoration from nearly 100 pictures of the car, the Purple People Eater Mk III was ready for its debut at Miller's 1993 "Corvettes at Carlisle" car show.

The interior was stripped but not devoid of stock gauges—even the clock remained!

Brought back to all its former glory, right down to the chromed wheels, roll bar, fuel-injected engine and yes, even the turnbuckle on the hood, original style decals and trim, the Purple People Eater Mk III proved to be that most defiant of all weeds—one continually fertilized by enthusiasm.

And the name? It was taken from a popular song written in 1958 by Ross Bagdasarian (later famous as David Seville

Interior of the PPE was stripped to the bare essentials for competition. Passenger seat was removable.

All of the dash instruments in Jefford's car were stock.

and the Chipmunks) and sung by none other than Sheb Wolly. "It was a one-eyed, one-horned, flying Purple People Eater. . ." The Nickey car had four blacked-out eyes, no horn, but it definitely flew!

Some Foreign Competition

Throughout the late 1950s and early sixties, the Lister works at Abbey Road in Cambridge, England, prepared Jaguars and Corvettes that were among the most respected race cars in European and American motorsports.

The Lister engineering firm built its first car in 1953, using a Tojeiro chassis and a modified 1,100 cc motorcycle engine. That design evolved into another in 1954, powered by

Driver Bob Edminson ran a Lister Corvette at Pomona in July 1962, and at the Los Angeles Times Grand Prix, in October 1962, car #24. (Photo by Dave Friedman)

an MG engine and yet another driven by a 2.0 liter six-cylinder Bristol. Lister produced the first Jaguar powered race car in 1957, on a new chassis of Lister's own design, fitted with a D-Type engine.

The Lister-Jaguars utilized a tubular frame chassis fitted with an aluminum body, which was supported by a lightweight steel tube framework (similar to the Maserati Birdcage).

The Listers were really small cars stretched just enough to accommodate larger engines, which accounted for their rather unusual body shape—massive fenders and bulging hoods, combined with a very low overall profile. In its first season, the Lister Jaguar, campaigned by works driver Archie Scott-Brown, won 12 out of the 14 races in which it was entered.

By 1958, Lister was producing cars for sale to privateer racers in Europe and in the United States, where the cars were imported with D-Type Jaguar engines or shipped without and fitted with Chevrolet V8s stateside.

Listers were imported through a small network of three distributors, all now very famous, Carroll Shelby, Kjell Qvale, and Alfred Momo. In all, some 20 to 30 cars were sold in the United States, and in fact, became quite popular among American racers after sportsman Briggs Cunningham took delivery of three Listers in 1958—two with D-Type Jaguar engines and one which was fitted with a Chevrolet V8. The three cars were prepared by Momo for Cunningham, and proceeded to win almost every event they entered.

Listers were driven in this country by Jim Hall, A.J. Foyt, Bob Edminson, Fred Windridge, and Chuck Daigh, among others. In Europe, they were being campaigned successfully by such distinguished teams as *Ecurie Ecosse* and *Equipe Nationale Belge,* along with drivers like Masten Gregory, Jim Clark, Scott-Brown and Bruce Halford. In a very short period, these hand built race cars earned an almost remarkable reputation that had taken other builders years, if not decades, to achieve.

Although the heyday of the Listers was short-lived, and ended tragically with the death of Lister's close friend and works driver Archie Scott-Brown in the Belgian Sports Car Grand Prix at Spa in 1958, the Lister Jaguars and Corvettes left their mark on motorsports history both here and in Europe.

The Grand Sport

Within Corvette racing lore, one name stands out above all others, the 1963 Grand Sport—a car largely the result of Carroll Shelby's success with the Cobra and Zora Arkus-Duntov's determination to beat them.

The GS is a subject GM management, circa 1960, would like to forget. Forget that Carroll Shelby offered the idea of combining a British-built AC Bristol with a big block American V8 to General Motors before going to Ford. Yes, the Cobra could have been powered by a Corvette engine. "What I wanted," said Shelby, "was a little 2,000 to 2,500 pound car. We could have done that by putting a lightweight body on the Corvette chassis, but the guys in charge of the Corvette program didn't think that was such a hot idea."

General Motors was holding fast to the Automobile Manufacturer's Association (AMA) doctrine signed in 1957, and in a decision which has haunted the halls of GM's Fourteenth Floor ever since, the world's largest automaker let Carroll Shelby slip between its fingers and into the grasp of arch rival Ford. Ford made an equally fallacious gaff when it let Shelby go to Chrysler back in the eighties. However, back in 1962, GM's errant decision, and its almost immediate repercussions, did not go unnoticed by the Sting Ray's engineering architect Zora Arkus-Duntov.

On October 16, 1962, Duntov's all-new Corvette Sting Ray made its competition debut at the *Los Angeles Times Grand Prix,* a three-hour invitational race, the very same at which Carroll Shelby and Ford Motor Company was invited to roll out the new Cobra. By the time the race was over, Duntov had witnessed an astonishing display of what sheer horsepower combined with lightweight bodywork could do. The normally aspirated Z06-optioned Sting Rays were simply

One of Lister's most famous drivers, A.J. Foyt, in the number 212 car at Daytona, April 1959. (Photo by Dave Friedman)

The U.S. marketing branch of Lister, Lister North America, produces custom bodies for current Corvette chassis.

no match for the Cobra. Even though the Corvette won, it was only through the grace of a broken wheel hub that the Shelby hadn't embarrassed the entire Chevrolet effort; of the four Zo6-equipped cars entered, only Doug Hooper's Sting Ray finished the race.

Although pleased with the victory, something brand-new production cars rarely achieved the first time out, Duntov was not blind to the reality of what had happened at Riverside.

"Although we won the first race, as far as I was concerned the writing was on the wall. Shelby will suffer loose wheels, loose axles, loose this and that, but ultimately he has the configuration which is no damn good to sell to the people, except very few, but by the looks of it will beat Corvette on the tracks unless we do something." And do something they did.

Duntov and Chevrolet General Manager Bunkie Knudsen quietly began development of a lightweight Corvette

The man and his machine. Designer-engineer Zora Arkus-Duntov and the 001 Corvette Grand Sport appeared together at the 1993 "Corvettes At Carlisle" event in Carlisle, Pennsylvania.

designed for competition. By the end of 1962, the Corvette Grand Sport, or "Lightweight" as Duntov called it, was in the testing stages at Sebring, and Knudsen was formulating a plan to build 125 cars for *Federation Internationalè de l'Automobile* FIA homologation, allowing the Corvettes to compete against Ford's 427 Cobras in 1963. This was 25 cars more than the FIA required for homologation, but Knudsen had decided that the additional Grand Sports would prove just how committed Chevrolet was. (Ferrari had soured the FIA early in 1962 with the 250 GTO, building less than 100 cars after receiving sanction.) Knudsen even envisioned going head to head with Ford in the showroom race, building a limited run of 1,000 Grand Sports to match Cobra production. It was not to be.

With anything less than a full-out effort on Chevrolet's part, Duntov and Knudsen reckoned that the FIA's *Championship of Manufacturers* would go to Ford in 1963, making the Cobra the first American car to win the coveted honor;

an exasperating vision for Knudsen, since the Cobra was at best only half American and barely a production car. The British-built ACs were modified by Shelby's general manager Peyton Cramer and his crew on makeshift assembly lines set up in two rented aircraft hangars at the Los Angeles International Airport. General Motors, however, after mulling over the situation, decided not to build any cars for competition in compliance with the AMA doctrine, even though Ford's Cobras blatantly flew in the face of the agreement, and Chrysler was pretty much repudiating it as well with factory supported car's like Bud Faubel's Dodge Hemi Honker. GM said no. Knudsen and Duntov went ahead regardless.

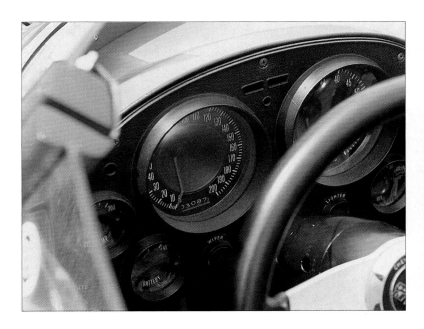

The Grand Sport's interior is functionally Spartan. Note the 200 mph speedometer and Duntov's signature on the dashboard.

The car that built the legend, the 001 Corvette Grand Sport developed by Zora Arkus-Duntov in 1963. The prototype coupe was redone by Duntov as a roadster for the 1964 season. Today it has been restored and painted in Penske colors by Doug Hooper. (Owner Gene Schiavone)

At first glance the first Grand Sport looked like a stylized Sting Ray, but a closer examination quickly belied any similarity beyond shape. On the exterior, the fenders were flared to cover wider tires, functional intake scoops were added to channel air to the brakes; the windows, except for the windshield, were replaced with Plexiglas, and the cars were fitted with a 36½ gallon fiberglass fuel tank, and a trunk. They were the only Sting Ray coupes ever equipped with a rear decklid.

Unlike the Cobra, which was a lightweight roadster from the start, the Corvette Grand Sport began with a production Sting Ray tipping the scales at around 3,100 pounds against the Cobra's lithe 2,000 pound curb weight. With better than a half ton disadvantage, Arkus-Duntov and his staff had to look in every possible area for ways to trim unsprung weight.

To reduce mass, the bodies were formed of thinner gauge fiberglass, three layers to a thickness of 0.040 in., and the steel birdcage structure of the production car was replaced with a hand-hammered sheet aluminum framework. The front upper and lower A-arms were built from sheet steel, instead of being stamped, the differential housing and steering box made of aluminum, and as many production components as possible replaced with lighter weight, hand-built equivalents. Anything that couldn't be replaced was drilled out, such as the rear suspension trailing arms.

The Grand Sport's suspension geometry approximated that of the production Sting Ray, which featured an all-new independent rear axle designed by Arkus-Duntov, Walter Zetye and Harold Krieger. Under the modified body was a ladder-type chassis constructed for the Grand Sport with massive tubular members that extended from front to rear. The tubes, made of seamless steel, connected at the front and back with cross-members of approximately the same diameter, while another tube crossed the middle of the chassis directly aft of the transmission. A fourth cross-member was added just ahead of the rear kick-up and served as the anchor point for an integral roll cage.

The chassis design was arguably makeshift, but the lightest possible Chevrolet could build short of a space frame, which simply was not in the Grand Sport's budget. . . It's difficult to allocate funds to a project you're not supposed to be doing! A few more pounds were shed by fitting the Grand Sport with 15 x 6 inch Halibrand knock-off magnesium alloy wheels.

Holes were cut into the back of the car to increase airflow. All of the Grand Sport Sting Rays had trunks, which was required by FIA regulations.

The Grand Sport still has the original inspection tag from the 1966 Sebring.

In the Grand Sport, the main chassis members ran directly under the cockpit, instead of alongside it, so the interior was slightly askew to production models and the driving position was somewhat higher. On the plus side, the body over frame design allowed quick removal of the fiberglass shell to facilitate repairs.

Having shaved as much weight as possible from the car, Arkus-Duntov and his team next tackled the Corvette's second biggest problem: brakes. In early tests, the Corvette's stock binders proved totally inadequate for competition. This was finally resolved with the adaptation of Girling four-wheel discs. However, even these needed to be modified. The stresses of scrubbing off racing speeds during field tests had the standard ½-inch rotors glowing red hot, so the final design utilized thicker 1-inch rotors. The new discs weighed only a

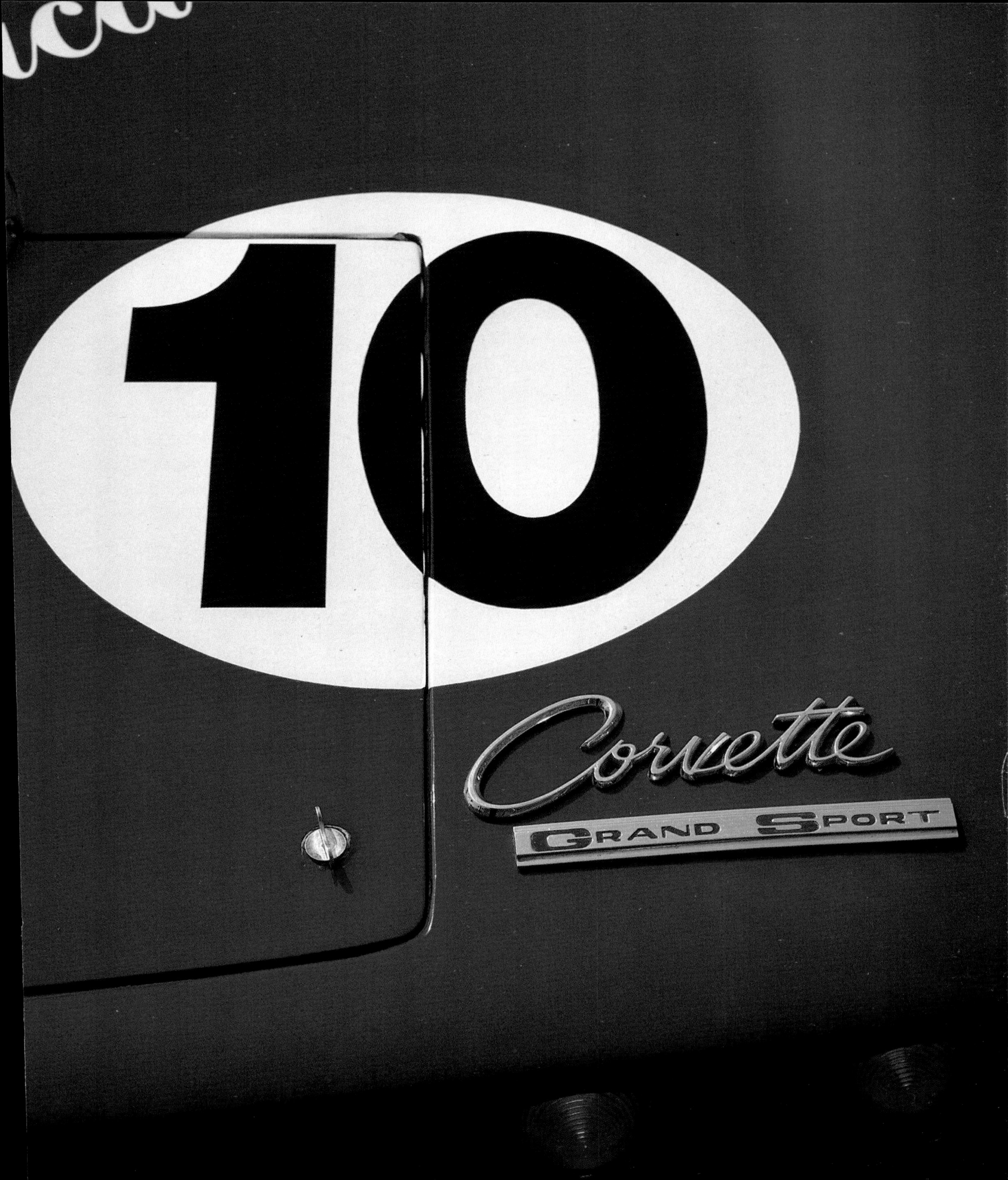
10
Corvette
GRAND SPORT

quarter pound more because they had internal venting passages that acted to pump air outward, like a centrifugal blower. The revised design lowered stressed braking temperatures by 100 degrees during repeated stops from 100 mph to rest at 0.8 g. deceleration.

When the prototype was finished, 001 weighed in at 2,341 pounds. Arkus-Duntov and Knudsen had met their goal. The Grand Sport weighed approximately the same as a Cobra.

Preliminary testing done at Sebring in December '62 caught the unwanted attention of GM management, which acted swiftly to issue a dictate bringing the program to an immediate end the first week of January 1963, what Duntov later referred to as "a screeching halt."

Though mortally wounded, the Grand Sport was not dead. Duntov and Knudsen continued the project within the Chevrolet Engineering Center using the parts that had been built before GM chairman Frederic Donner issued an internal memorandum to divisional chiefs ordering performance programs to stop. There were enough parts to build five cars.

The 001 Grand Sport is equipped with a Traco-built 427 engine and Holly carburetion, developing 560 bhp at 6400 rpm and a top speed of 152 mph.

Roger Penske and one of the three Grand Sport coupes that cleaned Shelby's clock in Nassau, December '63. (Photo by Dave Friedman)

The first Grand Sports to compete were equipped with modified iron block L-84 fuel-injected 327s, fitted with a special lightweight flywheel and clutch. Cars 001 and 002 were kept at Chevrolet, while 003 and 004 were campaigned "privately" by the Grady Davis team and Chevrolet dealer Dick Doane, in SCCA events held at Marlboro, Danville, Virginia, Cumberland, at Road America, Bridgehampton, and the Nationals at Watkins Glen.

Confined to the C-Modified class, the Grand Sports ran up against some pretty stiff competition like Lance Reventlow's Scarab and Jim Hall's Chaparral. Although the two coupes achieved only modest results, much was learned from the six month shaking out. The data was evaluated by Arkus-Duntov and used to modify the remaining cars at Warren.

Early in '63, Roger Penske had been called in to help "sort out" the Grand Sport's chassis. Working at the Waterford race course, just outside Detroit, Penske tested new wider tires, wheels and a variety of suspension modifications that would ultimately appear on the second generation Grand Sports campaigned at the 1963 International Bahamas Speed Week races by the John Mecom Racing team.

Three developmental Grand Sport coupes, 003, 004, and 005, painted in Mecom's Cadillac blue color scheme and powered by 377 cid aluminum engines, were "loaned" to the Mecom team—Penske, Dr. Dick Thompson, Jim Hall, and Augie Pabst—with technical support provided by Chevrolet engineers who just happened to be vacationing in Nassau!

The Corvette GS took all the venom out of Shelby's Cobras, besting the AC roadsters by nine seconds a lap. After the races, *Car and Driver's* Al Bochroch wrote: ". . . Chevy shot Ford right out of the sky at Nassau." In the Governor's Trophy race the Grand Sports came in 1-2-3 in class, as well as 3rd, 4th and 6th overall. Penske added a 1st in the prototype class to the week's victories, and the team scored 1st and 3rd in class and 4th and 8th overall in the International Nassau Trophy Race at the conclusion of Speed Week. Recalls Penske, "The Cobra was usually the Corvette's nemesis, but not at Nassau. We didn't have the brakes that the Cobra had, but the Lightweight was very responsive. It was quicker than the Cobras—quicker than the Ferraris, too." True, the Grand Sports would never race "officially" for Chevrolet, but everyone knew who had the fastest cars, just the same.

Back in Warren, Duntov had the prototype Grand Sport 001, and 002 coupes converted to roadsters for competition in the '64 Daytona Continental. The '64 season unfortunately never came. Publicity from the Grand Sport's victory in the Bahamas had GM management in a rage, and Knudsen was told in no uncertain terms that if he wanted to see a sharp cut in his year-end bonus, "keep racing." The ax fell hard. Chevrolet was to have absolutely nothing to do with racing or the Mecom team. Two of the coupes were summarily sold to John Mecom, Jr., and the third to Jim Hall. The two roadsters, still in engineering, were sold to Penske in 1966.

The Grand Sport coupes were raced privately in '64, and two of them, 003 and 005, returned to Nassau with Penske winning the big race in 005. The 1965 season was the Grand Sport's last hurrah as the coupes were modified by their respective owners and campaigned against newer and more sophisticated machines such as Ferrari's 330P4 and Ford's GT40 Mk IIB. The roadsters made their last assaults in 1966. The Penske 001 car, prepared for Sebring and driven by Dick Guldstrand and Dr. Dick Thompson, retired after sixty-five

laps and a serious shunt that finished much of the suspension, the exhaust system, and finally the engine. Repaired and readied for competition once again, 001 went to Mecom and later Jerry Hanna of Pasadena, Texas, who ran it in SCCA. Penske sold the 002 Grand Sport to friend and fellow racer George Wintersteen. He ran the car in SCCA competition and retired it after the '66 season. The 001 has been completely restored and today it is owned by Gene Schiavone of Essex, Connecticut.

The team to beat at Nassau was John Mecom's: Augie Pabst, Roger Penske, Dr. Dick Thompson, and Jim Hall, shown with one of the three "factory supported" Grand Sports. (Photo by Dave Friedman)

As race cars, the Grand Sports had great potential, should Arkus-Duntov been given the free hand he wanted. When I spoke with him last, Zora lamented that the cars never received the esteem they deserved until so many years later. They were unsung heroes orphaned by mandate. Even the tooling for the Grand Sports was destroyed. However, the one thing GM couldn't destroy was what Arkus-Duntov and Bunkie Knudsen had accomplished with the cars in 1963. They had defended the Corvette's honor and defeated the Shelby Cobras. They had, as historian Karl Ludvigsen wrote, ". . . served as a reminder to Ford that on the way up in its historic assault on the racing world, the way would not always be easy. [The Grand Sport] was also a marvelous morale-builder for the engineers at Chevrolet and the others in GM who felt that racing was not among the seven deadly sins."

Dick Gulstrand and Dr. Dick Thompson campaigned the Grand Sport at Sebring in 1966. The car retired after sixty-five laps and a serious shunt that finished much of the suspension, the exhaust system, and finally the engine. (Photo by Dave Friedman)

Engine:	Water-cooled V8 by Traco Engineering
Displacement:	427 cubic inches
Compression ratio:	11.0:1 (alternative ratios 10.0:1 and 12.0:1)
Carburetion:	Holly 4 bl.
Valve gear:	push-rod operated overhead valves, mechanical lifters.
Valve diameter:	Intake 2.20 in./Exhaust 1.72 in.
Power (SAE):	560 bhp @ 6400 rpm. (1.31 bhp per cubic inch)
Torque (SAE):	540 lbs/ft @ 5200 rpm
Transmission:	4-speed manual, all synchromesh
	1st: 2.21 69 mph @ 6500 rpm
	2nd: 1.64 92 mph @ 6500 rpm
	3rd: 1.27 119 mph @ 6500 rpm
	4th: 1.00 152 mph @ 6500 rpm
Wheelbase:	98.0 inches
Track F/R:	56.8/57.8 inches
Length:	172.8 inches
Width:	69.6 inches
Height:	51.9 inches
Ground clearance:	4.3 inches
Curb weight:	2341 pounds
Front Suspension:	Independent fabricated tubular unequal-length wishbones, combined coil spring/shock absorber units, anti-sway bar.
Rear Suspension:	Independent lower transverse leaf spring, half shafts acting as upper locating links, trailing arms, tubular hydraulic shock absorbers.
Steering:	Recirculating ball, 3.25 turns lock-to-lock.
Brakes:	Front 11.47-in. Girling discs with 3.30 x 2.04-in. pads (power assisted), Rear 11.50-in. Girling discs with 3.06 x 1.55-in. pads (power assisted).
Wheels:	8x15-in. magnesium knock-offs.

Doug Hooper takes the restored Corvette Grand Sport 001 through a shake down run prior to USRRC Series competition in 1993.

Chapter 4

Contemporary Competitors

The Corvette Challenge Cars

When Corvette enthusiasts say that no collectible Corvettes have been built since 1972, they are overlooking one of Chevrolet's greatest modern-day accomplishments—the 1988-'89 Corvette Challenge Series cars.

When the latest series Corvette was introduced in 1984, the heavyweight coupes immediately began dominating SCCA Showroom Stock competition. A nearly unbroken string of victories and four National Championships continued through 1987, and as the Corvettes kept winning, race teams and Chevrolet engineering steadily improved the car, further increasing its power, braking and handling ability. Corvettes were approaching g forces through the corners that were formerly the exclusive domain of Formula 1 race cars. However, this was only appealing to Chevrolet and legions of Corvette enthusiasts. By 1987, the other competitors in SCCA had had enough. They threatened to withdraw from the series, unless Corvettes were excluded. Hard to believe, but the SCCA caved in under pressure and, suddenly, the best showroom stock racer in the world was left without a series in which to compete!

Faced with a somewhat *unique* problem, Chevrolet took a page from IROC competition history. To keep the Corvette on the tracks and in the public eye, Chevrolet launched a showroom stock series of its own called the Corvette Challenge. Canadian John Powell, who initiated the Players Series for Firebirds and Camaros, was appointed as director of the series which began in 1988. It would be a test of driver skills and a showcase to prove what *basically showroom stock* Corvettes could do. To this end, all of the cars were identically built by Chevrolet and equipped by Protofab Engineering in Wixom, Michigan, with race seats, roll cages, fire systems, Desert Driveline low-restriction dual exhaust and other safety equipment. For competition, Dymag lightweight magnesium wheels with Goodyear Gatorbacks were used to help cool the brakes, which tended to overheat and lose efficiency during race conditions. PBR Automotive supplied special brake pads which could stand up to the extreme conditions of the all-out, one-hour sprints to the checkered flag. The conversions ran an estimated $15,000 over the price of a new Corvette Coupe.

Engines used in the Challenge Cars were all pulled by the Flint Engine plant, equalized within 2.5 percent of the stock 245 horsepower, and then sealed with tamper-proof paint that is visible only under a special light source. The cars were all weighed and all specifications checked and logged into a computer file that was carried to each event. Proof of the success of the equalization process was made evident by the lap times of the drivers. At track after track, 15 to 20 of the cars would post lap times within one second of each other! This put the onus on the drivers and made for some close and exciting competition.

The Challenge Cars were in effect *test beds* for Chevrolet. What broke or malfunctioned during competition was reviewed by Corvette engineers Doug Robinson and Frank Ellis. When the Challenge Cars arrived at a track, they underwent repeated examinations by Robinson, Ellis,

The white number 53 car was campaigned in 1988 by Jeff Andretti, Paul Tracy, and Jimmy Vasser. (Owner Chip Miller)

Johnny Rutherford campaigned the number 99 car for Young Chevrolet.

Chevrolet engineer Mike Dupree, and technicians from GM Cams equipped with new diagnostic equipment. Corvette engineers Julie Bellanti, Jack Gilles and Scott Alman, were also assigned to the Challenge Cars in the dual roles of "scrutineers" to keep the cars equal and running at peak levels, and "analysts" gathering data that would aid them in improving future production Corvettes. They conducted tests to determine if an engine had lost power, as well as spot any "creative power enhancements" performed by one of the teams.

The cars were equipped with Desert Driveline low-restriction dual exhaust systems for competition.

At the races, chassis engineers continually monitored ride height and suspension geometry to see that they were within stock specifications. All of their findings were logged into a computer record maintained for each car. In addition, the cars themselves had their own 256K RAM memory box with two internal boards capable of storing an entire race. Sensors wired information about various functions back to the memory box and after the race, the event could be replayed in detail to evaluate the performance of various components.

The chance to race new Corvettes in a relatively inexpensive series was irresistible to such drivers as movie star Bobby Carradine, Indy winner Johnny Rutherford, Jeff Andretti, Jimmy Vasser, Juan Fangio II, and top Escort Endurance drivers Tommy and Bobby Archer. A total of 56 1988 Corvette Challenge Cars were produced, though not all of them were actually campaigned. Some were held as backup cars and some were used as test cars.

For competition, Dymag lightweight magnesium wheels with Goodyear Gatorbacks were used to help cool the brakes, which tended to overheat and lose efficiency during race conditions.

When the Challenge Cars arrived at a track, they underwent repeated examinations by Corvette engineers, Julie Bellanti, Jack Gilles, and Scott Alman, who were assigned to the Challenge Cars in the dual roles of "scrutineers" to keep the cars equal and running at peak levels, and "analysts" gathering data that would aid them in improving future production Corvettes.

The 1988 Corvette Challenge Series consisted of ten 1-hour sprint races at well-known tracks, such as Riverside, Sears Point, Mosport, Road America, Mid Ohio, and others.

A $1,000,000 prize fund was raised from prime sponsors Mid America Designs, Goodyear Tire and Rubber Co., and Exxon. Each race paid out $50,000 in prize money and there was a $500,000 purse for an end-of-the season points fund.

With a fair amount of money at stake, there was no shortage of on-track action in Challenge Car competition, as ESPN learned in 1988, covering just a few of the races. The following year ESPN covered all of them! The identically equipped Corvettes and their equally matched drivers often turned the event into a *contact* sport, as cars jockeyed for position.

Much needed replacement parts were supplied by a trackside parts truck supervised by Mid-America Designs' Vice President, Steve Wiedman, and assisted by Butch Claar from Mid America's Motorsports Department. As the races were often only a week apart, eleventh-hour air shipments of parts were the rule rather than the exception; often parts warehouses could not supply the needed components in time. This brought Ed O'Keefe, an engineer at the Bowling Green Corvette Plant Action Center into the picture. He often came to the rescue with parts directly from the production line. Many late night and early morning runs to the local airports were necessary, but somehow, the needed items were found and bolted in place prior to the call of the starter's flag.

The majority of the 56 cars built in 1988 and the 29 produced the following year were independently sponsored, with many of them financed through Valley Chevrolet, in Wilkes-Barre, Pennsylvania. Individual Chevrolet dealers also got behind the Challenge Car program, such as Malcolm Connor in New Jersey, Crown Chevrolet, Tom Bell Chevrolet, Sunfair Chevrolet, Texas American Racing/Ninmicht Chevrolet, and Young Chevrolet. Corporations such as EDS, Sony, Stroh's, and many others also got on the sponsorship bandwagon as the Challenge Car Series gained momentum.

After the Series ended, some of the cars went back to their sponsors or owners, others to Valley Chevrolet where they were converted for street use; in fact, all of the Corvette Challenge Cars were converted back, "technically." At the end of the '89 season, Chevrolet—who *owned* the race motors—pulled them out of the cars in St. Petersburg, replacing the original L-98 engines. However, the competition motors were available to any owner wanting to keep them—all they had to do was cover the cost of shipping!

Since 1989, only a few Challenge Cars have changed hands, with each successive transaction raising the ownership stakes. The number 7 car, pictured, is owned by Chip Miller of Carlisle Productions, and this car is equipped with its original competition L-98 engine. Miller owns a total of five Challenge cars, including the '89 *backup car,* which was never raced, and a half interest in a sixth Challenge Car with Mid-America Designs' Mike Yager. "You'll probably find no more than four or five of the '88 series and only one or two of the '89 models available at any given time," says Miller, who paid $42,500 for the backup car in '89 and has since turned down twice that amount. "The people who buy these cars really want to keep them."

One of 50 cars campaigned in the $1 Million Sports Car Club of America challenge race for showroom stock 1988 models. Some of America's top drivers competed in the series which offered the biggest showroom stock purse in the history of SCCA.

Unlike vintage race cars, where documentation is often difficult to find, authenticating a Challenge Car is no problem. Chevrolet kept scrupulous records, every car is known, and there is a fraternity of ownership. In 1990 and again in 1995, a Challenge Car reunion took place at Carlisle. In addition, there is also a Challenge Car Registry which keeps track of all the cars. Unfortunately, it is only available to owners!

Miller, who is nothing short of a Corvette fanatic, (he usually has one sitting in his office!), says that there is a special synergy of sights and sounds which make the Challenge Cars unique. "They're loud! They're powerful and very streetable. That's a mixture that makes them desirable, very desirable," he said.

If one had to establish some kind of demographics for Challenge car owners, the most common thread would be age. "We're all between 40 and 55," observed Miller, "boy racers or men who aspired to be racers when they were boys."

As collectibles, the '88 and '89 Challenge Cars haven't reached Corvette Grand Sport status, and probably never will, as far as value. Where they excel is in the availability of parts to repair and maintain them. It is very easy to bring a car back to the condition it was in when it raced.

Miller, who has vintage-raced his '57 and '59 Corvettes, says that they do not feel as comfortable or as safe as the Challenge Cars. "I wouldn't want to put one upside down, but if I did, I feel certain I would walk away from it. I don't think you can say that about a '59."

The best aspect of the Corvette Challenge Cars is their practicality. Like Corvettes since the early fifties, you can drive it to the race track, suit up, take on the competition, and then drive it home. This is one of many attributes that have attracted club racers to the Corvette name for more than 35 years.

Pretty much a stock interior except for racing seats, roll cage, door netting, and fire extinguisher system. You could drive one of these cars to a race with the air conditioning on and the stereo playing!

The Number 7 Challenge Car has its original L-98 race motor. It was campaigned by Shawn Hendricks and Rippie Racing. (Owner Chip Miller)

The L-98 engines used in the Challenge Cars were all pulled by the Flint Engine plant, equalized within 2.5 percent of the stock 245 horsepower, and then sealed with tamper-proof paint that is visible only under a special light source.

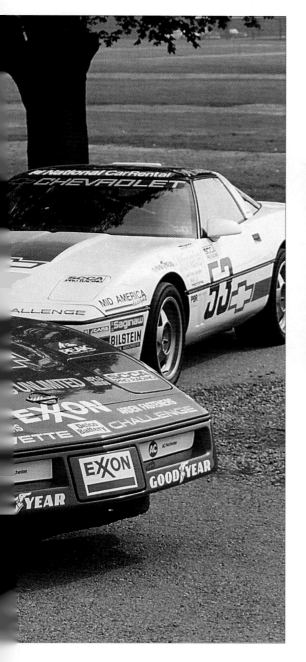

Only 56 cars were built in 1988 and 30 in 1989, making them a rare commodity. They seldom trade hands and their values continue to appreciate. It is estimated that '89 cars will one day reach $100,000 in value.

Chapter 5

A Million Cars Later

The Greatest Corvettes

Corvette generations spanning 35 years, the 1953 Corvette roadster and 1988 Corvette 35th Anniversary coupe.

Determination. It separates successes from also-rans. It sets the course of corporate achievement—the will to see a project through to its end. Today's Corvette is the result of such determination, an ideal that Chevrolet held to steadfastly, regardless of the economic climate or the actions of competitors.

In the fifties, Chevrolet could have followed Ford's lead, turning Corvette into another "Personal Luxury Car" as Thunderbird moved further away from its original Corvette-like concept. Instead, Chevrolet entrenched itself and continued to build a singularly dedicated two-passenger sports car.

The evolution of the Corvette since 1953 has brought sports car enthusiasts more than four decades of performance and excitement, cars that have literally become legendary in their own time.

As we stand on the threshold of the next century, it's interesting to look back at the Corvette's development and its changes over the past forty years.

When the Corvette first appeared in 1953 as part of GM's Motorama, an estimated four million persons viewed the car at appearances across the country and by the end of the year Chevrolet had hastily rolled out 300 Polo White Corvettes with sportsman red vinyl interiors, in answer to demands from dealers that "had to have that car in their showrooms."

By 1955 they were still in the showrooms. Unfortunately they were the '54 models. Sales had plummeted as sports car enthusiasts were rebuffed by the Corvette's shortcomings, and the public in general by its Spartan design and lack of traditional American car luxury features. . . like door handles. To cure part of the problem, in 1955 Chevrolet added a model equipped with a 265 cid, 195 hp V8 engine, fueled by a

One-million cars later, Zora Arkus-Duntov, (far right) and Chevy general manager Jim Perkins, congratulate assembly line workers as the millionth Corvette is completed. (Photo by Dennis Adler)

single four-barrel carburetor. Customers ordering the V8-equipped cars also got the added advantage of a 12-volt electrical system, and for the late part of the model year a 3-speed manual transmission was finally available as an option to the 2-speed automatic.

During 1954 and '55, Chevrolet Motor Division's chief engineer Ed Cole, Zora Arkus-Duntov, and chief stylist Harley Earl set about redesigning the Corvette from the ground up. Their first product appeared in 1956.

The contemporary body style, with convertible or removable hardtop, locking doors, roll up windows, and more comfortable interior was designed to meet the needs of those consumers who wanted comfort and convenience. And for the pure of spirit who had never felt Corvette offered sufficient power, beneath the new hood, Cole had placed a 265 cid V8 with a standard 210 hp output but engines as powerful 240 hp were available. A year later fuel-injection would be introduced and horsepower increased to 283; one hp per cubic inch with the top-of-the-line 283 cid V8. And to take full advantage of the added power, Corvettes could now be ordered with a 4-speed manual gearbox.

Before the millionth car left the line, Duntov slipped behind the wheel and started the engine. (Photo by Dennis Adler)

The first 300 Corvettes were hand-built on a pilot line at GM's Flint, Michigan, assembly plant. The first Polo White Corvette was completed on June 30, 1953. The Corvette was the world's first production car to be built with a Fiberglas body. On July 2, 1992, Chevrolet produced the millionth Corvette at the Bowling Green, Kentucky, plant.

By 1960, dual headlights had been adopted (first appearing in 1958) and Corvette was sporting a new grille design. Chevy also offered an optional 315 hp 283 cid V8 packaged with an exclusive 4-speed manual transmission. One of the most sought after options for 1960 was aluminum cylinder heads offered on fuel-injected cars. Very few were built with the aluminum heads, however, due to production problems dealing with casting high silicone aluminum. The option was deleted early in the model year. For 1960, Chevrolet sold a record 10,261 Corvettes.

The '61 and '62 model years marked several changes. They marked the transition, if you will, toward the next generation Corvette which would appear in 1963. A new grille design was introduced in '61, along with a reshaped tail section featuring four round taillights, a precursor to the '63 Sting

Ray. The '62 Corvette is perhaps one of the most desirable of all Corvettes. A car of many firsts and lasts. The first to use narrow whitewall tires, the first to feature rocker panel trim (which became a highlight of the next generation cars), and the first Corvette equipped with a 327 cid small-block V8. The '62 model was also the last to have a trunk, exposed headlights and marked the end of the solid axle Corvettes.

A new word and a new name for America's sports car came in 1963—Sting Ray. It was a radical departure from Corvette styling of the past. Under the watchful eye of GM stylist Bill Mitchell, the new Corvette had its roots in Mitchell's personal race car of the same name. The '63 models introduced independent rear suspension, concealed, rollover headlamps, arched fenders and a clean break with the European influence that had governed styling since 1953. For the first time Corvette came in two models, a convertible and the streamlined split window coupe. The ultimate version for '63 was the coupe, painted red, equipped with the Z06 option, knock offs, the 36 gallon fuel tank, fuel injection, and a 4-speed.

If you ever thought the '53 Corvette was a small car, just park it next to a new one!

Another milestone in Corvette history was the introduction of the Sting Ray in 1963. The unique body styling of the '63 'Vette set it apart from any other sports car in the world and it has become one of the most recognized automobiles of all time.

The '64 models were similar in design, except for the deletion of the rear window split which was determined to be an obstruction to visibility. Horsepower ratings reached an all time high for the small block achieving 375 with fuel injection.

While styling changed little in '65, Duntov was doing remarkable things mechanically. This would be the first year for four wheel disc brakes. The side louvers were made functional, and in mid year the MK IV engine came on line. A 396 cid cast iron motor unleashing 425 horsepower marked the beginning of big cubic inch motors and astronomical horsepower ratings. From a collector car standpoint, '65 was the only year the Corvette came with the 396. In following years the cars came with either a 427 or 454 cid V8.

In 1966, Chevrolet introduced the 427 V8 rated from 390 to 425 horsepower. Equipped with the 4-speed in close-ratio or heavy duty close-ratio gearing, heavy-duty brakes, special handling, and rear end options, the '66 Big Block

Another significant car in the evolution of the Corvette made its debut in 1968. Using designs from the Mako Shark II show car of 1965, the '68 models sported all-new exterior and interior styling, hidden headlights that popped up into position rather than rotating, concealed windshield wipers hidden under a vacuum-operated panel and a removable "T-top" on coupes, an industry first for production cars.

'Vettes became *King of the Road,* formidable on the street, respected on the road course and something to behold on the drag strip. These cars weren't driven, they were pointed in one direction and launched, with the driver holding on for the thrill of a lifetime!

The time for change came again in 1968. Corvette took on a new appearance and a new, even higher level of performance. As with the Sting Ray, the new Corvette closely resembled a Bill Mitchell concept car, this time the '65 Mako Shark II with pop-up headlights, removable T-Top roof panel and bold fenderlines. Under the hood, Chevrolet offered six optional engines ranging in output from 390 hp to 435 hp; however, the real killer option is the L-88 and L-71/89.

In 1969, Chevy broadened engine choices with the introduction of a 350 cid small block replacing the 327, and the ultimate limited production motor, the ZL-1, of which only two were made for the year!

Amid all the Big Block hoopla, in 1970 Chevrolet added a new small block to the Corvette option list, and one of the best engines in GM history, the 350 cid, 350 hp V8 with solid lifters, the now famous LT-1.

Chevrolet made news with another engine option, one which to this day still means absolute performance, the first ZR-1 factory-installed racing package. It includes the 350 cid LT-1 engine, a heavy-duty 4-speed, heavy duty power brakes, an aluminum radiator, special springs, shocks, and front anti-roll bar and rear spindle strut shafts. A total of eight were built. The '71 model year marked a turning point in American automotive history. This was the year all Corvette engines were designed to run on unleaded fuel. Things were about to change.

By the early seventies, Corvette was facing a competitor unlike any before. The 289 and 427 Cobras had been tough, but the Federal Government was tougher! Styling became more of a challenge with the introduction of impact bumpers in front for '73 and front and rear in '74. The GM design staff did yeomen work integrating the bumpers into the body and making them look good, but '74 was to be the swan song year for performance—the end of the 454 big block.

Throughout the mid- to late seventies, Chevrolet turned inward, making the Corvette more "personal," compensating for the lackluster performance with bells and whistles, leather and luxury. In 1977, Corvette had a restyled interior, a full line of Delco stereos available, and cruise control for the first time on a Corvette, (with automatic transmission).

The ZR-1 put all the excitement back into Corvette ownership that had been absent since the days of the 454 "big block" V8 and 400 plus horsepower. Adding 20 years for technology, the ZR-1 even with less than 400 hp could handily outrun the L-88 models of old and vanquish its 1971 namesake.

The ZR-1 was the epitome of Corvette performance, distinguished by a level of power that hadn't been seen in an American car for more than 25 years.

While there was still a good selection of suspension and handling packages, the once powerful Corvette engine was reduced to one optional 350 with 210 horsepower. By the end of the decade the weight of Washington was crushing Detroit.

It's hard to build a performance image in an era of non-performance, but Chevrolet managed in 1978, by celebrating its 25th Anniversary as the official pace car of the Indianapolis 500. The '78 model year was highlighted by the 25th Anniversary Edition Corvette, new fastback styling and a limited run of Indy Pace Car Replicas, which sparked a buying frenzy that to this day is a subject of conversation among Corvette enthusiasts and collectors alike.

Fuel efficiency, high tech, drag coefficient, and aerodynamics became industry buzzwords used to introduce the 1980 Corvette. A new low-profile hood, rear bumper cover incorporating an integral spoiler and black louvers over the fender vents were new styling features. Up front a new design increased air flow to the radiator and an air dam punctuated the body styling. The Federal Government, however, made a mockery of performance in 1980 by limiting speedometers to a maximum of 85 mph. Corvette owners simply read the tachometer! Under the hood was a 305 cid V8 for California (to meet California's emission requirements) and a 350 V8 for the rest of the country.

By 1971 the Stingray had become one of the most powerful street cars in the world. Optional "big block" engines offered up to 425 hp from a 454 cid V8. Only 12 cars were built with the 425/454 ZR-2 option, and 188 with the LS-6, both intended for competition, although a few found their way onto the nation's main streets. The rarest model in 1971 was the ZR-1, with a 330 hp, 350 cid engine. Only eight were produced.

The 1974 model year was another turning point, although not one remembered as a benchmark in Corvette history. It saw the demise of the 454 cid V8 and the introduction of body-color, integrated rear bumpers to match the integrated front bumpers introduced the previous year. The Corvette looked longer and heavier than ever before and as Federal regulations began to cut the heart out of performance cars, the Corvette began to change its image.

Although the styling on the 1975 Corvette appears the same as 1974, a new integral honeycombed, energy-absorbing bumper system is used both front and rear. It is the first year for the catalytic converter and the last year for a Corvette convertible.

OFFICIAL PACE CAR
62nd ANNUAL INDIANAPOLIS 500 MILE RACE
MAY 28, 1978

For 1978, Corvette was chosen to pace the 62nd Indianapolis 500 Mile Race. Chevrolet commemorated the event by producing 6,502 Black and Silver Indy Pace Car replicas, at least one for every Chevrolet dealer in the country. The cars could be ordered complete with official Indy 500 Pace Car decals.

A change in styling brings Corvette a much needed image boost. The new fastback design coincides with Corvette's 25th year of production and a special silver anniversary badge replaces the traditional crossed-flags emblem.

Chevrolet was making every effort to give the Corvette some added horse-power as emissions standards continued to choke performance out of most cars. For '79 the base 350 cid L-48 engine gained roughly 10 hp through the use of a new "open flow" muffler design to reduce back pressure and a low-restriction, dual-snorkel air intake, previously used on just the optional L-82 225 hp, 350 cid engine.

By the early eighties the basic Corvette shape introduced in 1968 was getting a little long in the tooth for just about everyone, especially Chevrolet, which was hard at work on a new generation of cars planned for a 1983 introduction. The 1982 model was to be the last of the old guard, equipped with a 5.7 liter V8 featuring Crossfire Injection. There was no manual transmission available but Chevy introduced a new 4-speed automatic. Since this was to be the farewell year for the Sting Ray body design, Chevrolet produced a special "Collector's Edition" featuring the first-ever lifting glass hatchback and a standard L-83 200 hp V8.

The rarest Corvette of the eighties, one of the 16 hand-built 1983 models pacing a '63 'Vette at Riverside Raceway. All 16 cars were kept by GM.

Testing at Riverside International Raceway in 1983, a prototype model planned for European export. (Photo by Dennis Adler)

In 1983 Chevy rolled out a handful of prototype models, this one poised alongside one of the original 300 Corvettes built 30 years before. (Photo by GM Photographic)

By 1984, the time for change had come once again, both for styling, and mercifully, for performance. Acceleration, speed, and horsepower were no longer ineffable. In 1983, for all intents, there was no Corvette, '82 models were continued until the Bowling Green plant completed tooling for the all-new 1984 models. However, Chevrolet did produce 16 hand-built 1983 prototypes, all of which belong to GM. The new, next generation Corvette hit the streets as an early 1984 model and the current model line has become the most successful in Corvette history.

With the return of the Corvette convertible in 1986, the lineage came full circle. Once again there were coupe and convertible versions, and from 1990 until 1995, the ZR-1 rekindled the great high-performance days of the late sixties and early seventies. Even though 1995 marks the end of ZR-1 production, the Corvette's future is more promising than ever.

One of the Official Pace Car replicas from 1986, marking the second time Corvette was honored by the Motor Speedway and the return of the Corvette convertible. (Photo by GM Photographic)

Where Corvette styling will go in the future is still undecided. The current body design will likely be with us until 1997. The challenge of changing the Corvette has always been difficult; over the decades since Harley Earl's first design, there have been many proposals. Some led to future generations, others led to never realized possibilities. The once and future American Sports Car will always be there.

An added touch offered in 1988 was the Z-51 optioned GTO model with special ground effects and rear decklid spoiler. A special order option—very few were produced.

It was to be the ultimate Corvette. Introduced as a 1990 model, the ZR-1 set new performance standards with a 375 hp, 4-cam, 32- valve, 90 degree LT-5 V8 engine developed jointly by Chevrolet and Lotus. The body was subtly different from other Corvettes, although the bodywork was a preview of 1991 Corvette styling. When the ZR-1 went on sale it became an instant premium, and for many owners it was worth every penny over retail. Produced through the 1995 model year, it will likely go down in history as the greatest Corvette since the 1960s (Photo by Dennis Adler for Chevrolet Motor Car Division of General Motors).

The need for speed has always kept tuners gainfully employed, but no one did for Corvette what Carroll Shelby did for Mustang until Reeves Callaway came along. His latest model, the Callaway SuperNatural Corvette LM, takes styling to the next level and blends it with Callaway's proven Super Natural-modified 6.3 liter, 435 hp, Corvette engine. The body is a race proven design by Callaway stylist Paul Deutschmann, tested under fire in the 24 Hours of Le Mans in 1994 and 1995.

The '96 Callaway LM has a custom hand-sewn leather interior that rivals the best from Europe.

Callaway's 1996 LM model features an aerodynamic nose with enclosed headlights, oval air intake (reminiscent of Jaguar and Ferrari designs from the 1960s), and dual brake cooling ducts.

One of the original nine Series I Callaway Speedsters built on the L-98 Twin-Turbo platform. The Limited Edition Series II Speedsters are based on the Callaway Super Natural Corvettes introduced in 1992.

The Corvette convertible regained its fame as America's fastest and most stylish open car. A stock 'Vette convertible was capable of a 145 mph top end and zero to 60 in under 6 seconds with the new ZF 6-speed manual transmission.

The new dashboard introduced in 1990 was a modern-day takeoff on the cockpit styling first seen in the 1963 Corvette. A removable hardtop, introduced in 1990, also captured a touch of sixties era styling. (Photos by Dennis Adler for Chevrolet Motor Car Division of General Motors.)

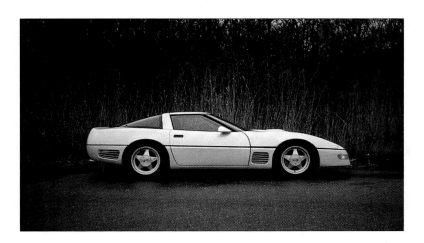

Back in 1987 Chevrolet added a new RPO number to the Corvette catalog, "B2K" and with it came an entirely new generation of models, the Callaway Corvette. Just as Carroll Shelby had done with Ford Mustangs in the sixties, Reeves Callaway, in Old Lyme, Connecticut, was now tuning and modifying production Corvettes, cars that could be ordered from any Chevrolet dealer in the country. The '87 Callaway had an output of 435 hp, 465 lb. ft. torque, and blistering top speed of 177.9 mph. Originally, the bodywork consisted of subtle changes but by the early nineties, Callaway Corvettes had a look all their own, as easily identifiable as a Shelby G.T. 500 was in 1967. The models pictured are a 1991 SuperNatural convertible and '92 coupe.

149

The modern day Corvette has managed many changes since 1984, from wheels and interior redesigns to new, more aggressive front and rear body panels, but the early design, like those pictured, still holds the most attraction because it was the first of the breed, the latest generation in its purest form. The Corvette convertible, however, more than any model, even the ZR-1, captures the allure of the original Corvette, an open air, free-spirited car described by Ken Purdy as ". . .an automobile built for the sole purpose of going like a bat out of hell. . ."

The LT-5, 4 cam, 32-valve V8 engine has become one of the most highly regarded engine designs in American automotive history.

Back in 1958, Harley Earl's long time protégé—Bill Mitchell—designed a running concept car called the XP 700. The XP 700 "Dream Car" ultimately led to the design of the '61 and '62 Corvette models. Mitchell and his staff had blended a variety of ideas, old and new, to shape the XP 700. The outcome, however, was a rear fender treatment that evolved into the '61 and '62 models and served as the foundation for the rear treatment on the all-new '63 Sting Ray. Sometimes getting that much out of a concept car was a lot.

Chapter 6

A Designer's Sketchbook

A Look Back at Forty Years of Design

Concept. The name given to cars that are experimental models—no more than test beds for new ideas, engineering technology, or design proposals. Most end up as scrap and are never seen or heard of again. Occasionally, one is found resting on flaccid tires, fading away in the corner of a dusty shuttered garage, and it is immediately elevated in stature by enthusiasts from ancient junk to that of treasured artifact—as if a sealed chamber had been opened to reveal the relics of an extinct civilization. Usually what is uncovered is the skeleton of a failed project, a curiosity at best.

Throughout the last 40 years, there have been more than a dozen Corvette concept cars, most of which were merely "styling exercises" and auto show exhibit cars. Some, however, have been the basis for new models—the foundation, if you will, for future generations of Corvettes.

The GM Design Studio, once called the Art & Colour Section, when the great Harley Earl was General Motors' chief of inspiration, has turned out countless concept cars, many of which led to production models. Keeping good company with the Corvette, originally designed by Earl in 1952, are models like the first Cadillac Eldorado Brougham, the Chevy Nomad, and the Buick Riviera.

Back in 1958, Harley Earl's long time protégé, Bill Mitchell, designed a running concept car called the XP 700. Mitchell had just taken over from Earl as Chief of GM Styling. The XP 700 "Dream Car" ultimately led to the design of the '61 and '62 Corvette models. The dual headlights and fender treatment, rocker panel trim, and new Sting Ray style rear end all evolved from this car.

While Corvette enthusiasts were taking in the sporty lines of the new '61 models, Mitchell and the design staff were building the Mako Shark, which in turn influenced the styling of the all-new 1963 Corvette. In '65, the Mako Shark II set the styling pace for the '68 model line. The aggressive look of the

While Corvette enthusiasts were taking in the sporty lines of the new '61 models, Mitchell and the design staff were building the Mako Shark I, which in turn influenced the styling of the all-new 1963 Corvette. This was probably one of the most telling of Mitchell's concept cars because so much of he Sting Rays's body lines were depicted. The concept cars were, of course, always a little over the top so as not to give too much away. Although, the quad exhaust pipes and shark-like nose might not have been bad!

fourth generation 'Vette was there in the Shark's muscular profile and bold front end design. One feature that never went past the concept stage was the car's unique *fade-away* paint scheme which duplicated the body coloring of a shark!

Of course, not every Corvette Concept car led to the design of a new model. If it had, the Astro I, introduced in 1967, would have put GM light years ahead of the competition. The Astro I featured Chevrolet's "flowback roof" design.

In '65, Mitchell came up with his proposal for the next generation Corvette. Replacing the '63 Sting Ray was not an easy task, as it had become one of the most popular cars on the road. Mitchell took his original Mako Shark concept and carried it to the next level, Mako Shark II, what would eventually become the 1968 Corvette. The aggressive look of the fourth generation 'Vette was there in the Shark's muscular profile and bold fender lines, the shape of the greenhouse. As time went on, even the contours of the shuttered rear window would evolve into the Corvette fastback design introduced in 1978.

Sometimes idea cars were just that, ideas. The Astro I featured Chevrolet's "flowback roof" design with an electric swing-back roof, instead of doors, and a rear section combined with power elevator seats that allowed the driver and passenger to step right into the car and sit at armchair height.

The car had an electric swing-back roof, instead of doors, and a rear section combined with power elevator seats that allowed the driver and passenger to step right into the car and sit at armchair height. At the push of a button, the occupants were lowered to a semi-reclining position beneath the roof, which closed down to a height of only 35½ inches.

The Astro I was powered by an air-cooled, single overhead camshaft six-cylinder engine.

Another Corvette Concept that toured the auto show circuit in the late sixties was Astro II. In 1968, Chevrolet wrote: "The Astro II idea car will be a special feature in this year's auto show. The contours of the car accommodate wide section tires which promote stability and handling, and reflect the change in dimensions which result from the mid-wheel base location of the engine, a liquid-cooled V8. The Astro II carries its radiator at the rear, a location intended to minimize the amount of plumbing required and to keep the hot water lines from passing through the passenger compartment. This arrangement frees the front compartment for luggage storage. The car was designed for Chevrolet by General Motors Design Staff." More than almost any other advanced concept car built during the late sixties, Astro II came closest to production quality appearance and at one time was thought to be the next Corvette. Ultimately, it proved to be just one of several ideas, none of which ever saw the light of day.

Chevrolet was still thinking about a mid-engine sports car when it proposed the "4-Rotor" in the early seventies. This was yet another possible replacement for the fourth generation 'Vette. It incorporated a totally new body design, "Gullwing-type" doors and a Chevrolet-Wankle rotary engine, mounted amidships.

The engine boasted a displacement of 585 cubic inches with an output of 350 hp at 7000 rpm. When GM's rotary engine development ended, the car was fitted with a V8 and renamed the Aerovette.

Cars like the Astro II and 4-Rotor could have changed the entire course of Corvette styling and engineering had their designs been adopted. In general, such wide sweeping changes seldom occur. Change, like aging, is usually gradual. Concept cars like today's CERV III point the way to the future. Not an absolute future, but one possible future among many.

Other times, designs were given serious consideration. The Astro II made the car show circuit in 1968, proposing a mid-engine Corvette replacement, although technical problems with a proper transaxle had the mid-engine proposal idling within GM. The Astro II featured contours designed to accommodate wide section tires which promoted stability and handling, and reflected the change in dimensions which resulted from the midships engine location. More than almost any other advanced concept car built during the late sixties, Astro II came closest to production quality appearance and at one time was thought to be the next Corvette.

Chevrolet was still thinking about a mid-engine sports car when it proposed the "4-Rotor" in the early seventies. This was yet another possible replacement for the fourth generation 'Vette. It incorporated a totally new body design, gullwing-type doors, and a Chevrolet-Wankle rotary engine, mounted amidships.

As little as five years ago, GM was still considering a mid-engine replacement for the Corvette. The CERV III was developed by Chevrolet-Pontiac-Canada Group's advanced vehicle engineering group. Many of the systems proposed on the CERV III (Corporate Experimental Research Vehicle) may find their way into the next generation Corvette, although the idea of placing the engine amidships is still not one of them. The CERV III was a running prototype powered by a 5.7 liter, 650 hp twin-turbocharged and intercooled 32-valve V8 with aluminum block and heads.

Chevrolet's latest concept car, the Sting Ray III, incorporates the best of past Corvettes while surging into the future. Designed at GM's Advanced Concept Center, Sting Ray III features dramatically angled headlights, pedals that move with a memory to preset positions, a wheelbase nearly seven inches longer, at 103 inches, than current production Corvettes, yet Sting Ray III's overall length is two inches shorter. While there are no comments from Chevrolet that this is The Look *for the next generation Corvette to be introduced in 1997, past history tells us that Chevy concept cars are often a good indication of forthcoming styles!*